Grammar and Writing

Series Editor: DR REBECCA STOTT

SPEAK
WRITE
SERIES

Other titles in the series:

Writing with Style

Rebecca Stott and Simon Avery (Eds)

Speaking your Mind: Oral Presentation and Seminar Skills

Rebecca Stott, Tory Young and Cordelia Bryan (Eds)

Making your Case: A Practical Guide to Essay Writing

Rebecca Stott, Anna Snaith and Rick Rylance (Eds)

Grammar and Writing

Edited by Rebecca Stott and Peter Chapman

Series Editor: Rebecca Stott

An imprint of **Pearson Education**

Harlow, England · London · New York · Reading, Massachusetts · San Francisco · Toronto · Don Mills, Ontario · Sydney
Tokyo · Singapore · Hong Kong · Seoul · Taipei · Cape Town · Madrid · Mexico City · Amsterdam · Munich · Paris · Milan

Pearson Education Limited
Edinburgh Gate
Harlow
Essex CM20 2JE
England

and Associated Companies throughout the world

Visit us on the World Wide Web at:
www.pearsoned.co.uk

───────────────

First published 2001

ISBN-10: 0-582-38241-6
ISBN-13: 978-0-582-38241-1

British Library Cataloguing-in-Publication Data
A catalogue record for this book is available from the British Library

Library of Congress Cataloging-in-Publication Data
Grammar and writing / edited by Rebecca Stott and Peter Chapman.
    p. cm. — (Speak-write series)
  Includes bibliographical references and index.
  ISBN 0-582-38241-6 (pbk.)
    1. English language—Grammar—Problems, exercises, etc. 2. English
  language—Rhetoric—Problems, exercises, etc. I. Stott, Rebecca. II. Chapman,
  Peter. III. Series.

  PE1112.G674 2000
  808'.042—dc21   00-032125

10 9 8 7 6 5 4
08 07 06

Typeset by 35 in 10.5/12.5 Janson
Printed and bound in Malaysia, GPS

CONTENTS

AUTHOR'S ACKNOWLEDGEMENTS

This book and the other three books in the Speak–Write Series, *Writing with Style, Speaking Your Mind: Oral Presentation and Seminar Skills,* and *Making Your Case: A Practical Guide to Essay Writing,* have been three years in the making. They are the result of three years of research, teaching design and piloting undertaken by the Speak–Write Project, established by the English Department of Anglia Polytechnic University in Cambridge and funded by the Higher Education Funding Council for England through its Fund for the Development of Teaching and Learning. The Speak–Write Project was set up to respond to claims from members of English departments across the country that first-year undergraduates needed more intensive advanced writing and speaking courses at foundation level in order to perform more effectively in higher education.

Although the Speak–Write Project looked closely at freshman rhetoric and composition classes which have run successfully in the United States for decades, the Speak–Write designers and researchers concluded that there was a need in British higher education for innovative communication skills courses which were embedded in specific subject areas and not generic skills courses alone. These four books have been piloted, designed and adapted by and for lecturers and students working in English Literature departments and much of the material presented for analysis or rewriting or adaptation is of a literary kind. This said, the books have a much wider application and can be adapted for use by a range of cognate disciplines in the Humanities.

The Speak–Write books have drawn on the imaginations, time and work of many people. The editors and authors of individual books and chapters are acknowledged beneath the chapter and book titles. Many more people and institutions have contributed who remain invisible and I would like to thank as many of them individually here as possible: Tory Young, Editorial

Assistant, who saw the books through their final metamorphosis, tirelessly and with great good humour and editorial skill; Ruth Maitland, the Speak–Write Project's Administrator, who held everything together; Rob Pope (Oxford Brookes University), Stephen Minta (York University), Val Purton (City College, Norwich), Morag Styles (Homerton College, Cambridge) and Katy Wales (Leeds University), the External Readers who assessed and advised on early drafts of the books; Paul Boyd, Richard James, Regine Hasseler, Shelby Bohland and Lucy Wood, the student editorial advisory group; Elizabeth Mann, Commissioning Editor at Longman, for her encouragement and enthusiasm for the Project in its early stages; staff and students of the English Department at Anglia Polytechnic University who have refined and shaped the books through giving continual feedback on aspects of teaching and learning; and my first-year students of 1999 in particular for applying their creative minds to difficult editorial decisions.

Rebecca Stott, *Series Editor*

PUBLISHER'S ACKNOWLEDGEMENTS

We are grateful to the following for permission to reproduce copyright material:

The Crown's Patentee, Cambridge University Press for extracts from 'Genesis' ch. 9, verses 15–19 the Authorised Version of the Bible (*The King James Bible*), *the rights in which are vested in the Crown*; Channel 4 Television for transcript of extract from *BOOKED* a Channel 4 programme shown in December 1998; Rob Pope for transcript in Chapter 1; Random House Group Ltd/the author's agent for an adapted extract from *CHARLES DICKENS* by Peter Ackroyd published by Sinclair-Stevenson; Wine & Dine e-zine for an extract from the article 'Recipes from the French Wine Harvest' by Clifford Mould from www.winedine.co.uk. The table in Chapters 1 and 2 is reprinted from *REDISCOVER GRAMMAR*, 205, © Longman Group UK Ltd., with permission from Pearson Education Limited, (David Crystal, 1988).

We have been unable to trace the copyright holder of 'The Story' from *FROG AND TOAD ARE FRIENDS* by Arnold Lobel and would appreciate any information that would enable us to do so.

INTRODUCTION

Rebecca Stott and Peter Chapman

This is a practical book. Its central aim is to help you to develop and improve your writing skills from the point you are at now. Not everything in this book is *directly* practical, however. We take you through some language analysis and frequently comment upon what we call language awareness, but these topics are a means to an end: they feed into the central focus of the book, which is the activity of writing.

More specifically the book is about the links between grammar and writing. Many people have bad memories of struggling with grammar at school and so the prospect of learning about 'grammar and writing' may be a gloomy one. Why do we need to explore grammar in a book which aims to develop writing skills? The answer is that grammar is the organising principle of language. If writing is a craft, writers need to know the materials they are working with and the tools they are going to use.

You already 'know' a great deal of grammar because, as you are using the English language to communicate with others, you have already mastered thousands of intricate structures and exceptions to those structures without even noticing that you have learnt them. But if you are to understand where your writing can be improved and gain greater awareness in the many varieties of writing, you will need to find a way to describe what you are doing when, for instance, you put a group of words together to make a sentence. This book aims to give you that metalanguage (the language used to describe language; 'meta' comes from the Greek word for above) and to help you to develop your writing through constant practice and an increased awareness of what you are doing when you write for different purposes.

One of our main assumptions in this book is that ignoring the ways in which language structures work can lead to vague, impressionistic reading and somewhat scrappy writing. So although this is a book concerned with *practical* writing skills, and not primarily a grammar book, we aim to give you just enough knowledge of grammar (or the structures of language) to help you develop your writing. We are not concerned with the finer points of grammatical theory. There are many excellent grammar books available which will explain these things in detail and we have included a list of these in the further reading section.

The word 'grammar' derives originally from a Greek word which means a 'letter' i.e. 'of the alphabet'. You might be surprised that it does *not* derive from a word meaning 'rules of correct language'. So if we restricted ourselves to the original definition, then 'grammar' would mean studying how letters are combined to make words. Thus 'grammar' meant studying the organisation of the structures of *written* language. It is easy to see, though, that *spoken* language also follows patterns and structures – not exactly like written language admittedly – and so grammar should finally come to mean studying how language as a whole is organised and structured.

Where, then, did the idea that grammar means speaking (and writing) *correctly* come from? This interpretation of grammar as 'rules for correct English' is the one that has given it a bad name. It is the reason why all of us, including the authors of this book, are a little wary of the word. After all, if we generally succeed in communicating with others verbally then knowledge and use of mysterious grammatical principles can seem pointless. Perhaps what seems most objectionable about this widespread notion of grammar as 'rules for correct English' is the implication that one form of language is always appropriate and other forms are always incorrect and inferior.

However, as language evolves with the people who speak and write it there will always be debates about language use as it changes: debates between those who want to stick to rules derived from the study of ancient languages, particularly Latin (a 'dead' language, of course, but a highly influential one), and those who see such rules as relative, and language as fluid. Ironically, it is often the language experts who are more tolerant of linguistic idiosyncrasies than some members of the general public. The 'split infinitive', for instance ('to boldly go', rather than 'to go boldly'), is now generally regarded to be acceptable, but there are a number of Radio Four listeners who write in to complain every time they hear one used on the radio. Very few people, however, would argue in favour of abandoning all conventions of usage, because structures of language are in place in order to facilitate communication. We need agreement in order to be able to understand each other and we need to have some way of describing the structure of sentences in order to assess and develop our writing and clarity.

Context plays a fundamental role in language – so fundamental that we could call it the first principle of language awareness. Take the two questions: 'To whom am I speaking?' and 'Who am I speaking to?'. Which is 'correct' or 'incorrect'? The former is generally considered the more 'correct', but is probably not used by most people. Perhaps this degree of formality would be appropriate for, say, the United Nations telephone exchange, but almost rude if you are ringing the family home of your best friend. Similarly, if you called your best friend and said 'Me and Mark are going into town, do you want to come?' and he replied 'Actually, you should say "Mark and I"', you might be tempted to withdraw your offer and invite someone less pedantic instead. Absolute 'correctness' is then a questionable value; on the other hand, 'appropriateness', to context, and to communicative purpose, is a much more useful idea. Most in-built computer grammar-checkers will first ask you what kind of document you are writing, because these programmes also make a distinction between grammatical conventions for formal or informal writing.

Grammar books, however, can be divided into three main categories: prescriptive grammar books which set out rules (although these are hard to find now and will probably be reprints of books written much earlier last century), descriptive grammar books which describe all the patterns and variations without being dogmatic, and selective grammar books which do not try to cover everything but only what they consider to be the necessary grammatical structures for their chosen context. This book is a selective grammar book because we are exploring grammar in practical terms, as part of the process of writing. It also sets out to explore grammar in relation to literary and non-literary published writing and writing in process. It is explorative rather than prescriptive.

In this book we stress that language and conventions of writing must be flexible to allow for the fact that people write for different purposes. We can talk about the rules or conventions for degree-level essay writing, for example, without implying that these rules apply to all writing which involves argument and point of view. Just because a narrow, rigid and often inhibiting view of grammar as the 'rules' of correct language has been widespread, do not be tempted to reject the idea of them completely, but be sure to rethink what you mean by 'rules'. This is one of the things we shall be doing in this book.

We will also explore grammar and style. These two aspects of language study are often kept separate. We cannot follow this practice because we wish to explore *how stylistic purposes determine grammatical choices*. We are interested in what we would call 'different grammars' of different styles and varieties of writing. In real life, we are always using, and shifting between, one or other of the varieties or styles of language that our cultures make available to us. We may write an e-mail to a friend, a note to a flatmate, an essay, and a formal letter to a bank manager all in the course of a day. Each will require different styles of written English and different decisions about the grammatical structures available to us. In this book we have made a selection from the whole network of the structures (the grammar) of English. We concentrate on those forms and uses we think you need to be aware of for both your writing and your reading. We have also selected many different pieces of writing from literature, journalism, advertising and academic writing in order to look at the relationship between grammar and style in these varieties of written English.

How to use this book

As you carefully work through the sections of the book, and the sequences of steps and examples in each section, you will be developing both your language awareness and your writing skills as you proceed. We have built into each section a number of writing activities. There will be word, phrase and sentence exercises but we will also offer you the chance to analyse and imitate, either closely or quite freely, the styles of existing writers, some of them famous, because we believe that *doing* is one of the most effective methods of learning.

As you work through the book, you may find that some material is familiar to you. If so, you can afford to work more swiftly through such parts; but we would advise you not simply to 'skip', as we would like you to be aware of the approach we take to all the topics we deal with, as well as how we relate all our topics and levels of language to each other. We have structured the book very carefully and progressively and we will often be referring back to parts we have already covered and forward to items not yet dealt with. Broadly speaking then, we are advising you not just to *read*, but to *work through* the sequences of steps and examples from Chapters 1 to 7. Some of the activities will be more demanding (in terms of time and level of difficulty) than others. Most chapters have about ten to twelve activities to complete, each of which will enhance your understanding of the material in the chapter in different ways.

We hope our presentations, explanations and illustrations are clear and practically useful. If you work attentively and systematically through this book, your language awareness will be increased in a number of ways, and you will be able to carry out the writing tasks with success and, we hope, enjoyment. After working through the selected grammar in this book you will, if you wish to, or need to, be able to consult fuller grammars of English and to do so with confidence about where to look and what to look for. If, as Ludwig Wittgenstein claimed, 'The limits of [your] language stand for the limits of [your] world', then increasing your knowledge of language can only expand your world.

Making sense of sentences

Rebecca Stott and Peter Chapman

A closer knowledge of grammatical structures will help you to appreciate and analyse the skills of other writers as well as help you to structure, edit and polish your own sentences more effectively. In *A Room of One's Own* (1929) Virginia Woolf describes picking a novel randomly from her bookshelf and trying 'a sentence or two on [her] tongue' in order to find out whether the novelist 'has a pen in her hand or a pickaxe'. Getting a feel for sentences involves many senses, as Woolf suggests, and being able to understand a sentence grammatically will sharpen your writing and reading senses in interesting and useful ways. Hearing, feeling, 'tasting' and seeing the patterns and structures of language reveals the infinitely variable and subtle stylistic effects that individual writers create.

Recognising grammatical structures

Is it possible just to write, with no rules or aims or readers in mind? Is it possible just to let the pen or the cursor go with no control of what will be produced? Surrealists in France in the 1920s thought it was and they even thought that the result, not being contaminated by the thought of readers, the 'society in our heads', would be more valuable than writing produced by conscious calculation. They called this spontaneous kind of writing *automatic* writing.

Here is a later example of experimental writing that appears to be automatic writing but is in fact very carefully crafted to give the effect of a kind of stream-of-consciousness (as though we could hear someone's thoughts directly). It comes from 'How It Is', a late work of Samuel Beckett, the novelist and playwright, written in the 1960s:

> the voice quaqua on all sides then within in the little vault empty closed eight planes bone-white if there were a light a tiny flame all would be white ten words fifteen words like a fume of sighs when the panting stops then the storm the breath token of life part three and last it must be nearly ended . . .

(Beckett 1973: 179)

Beckett is experimenting with language to create an effect of panic and hopelessness, evoking perhaps the consciousness of a man trapped inside his own body nearing death. In these short pieces Beckett assembles words into some kind of pattern, but not into any grammatical pattern *at the level of sentences*; nor is there any punctuation. The words do cluster in interesting ways, though, and there are recognisable phrases and other word groups which stand out and are fully grammatical: 'like a fume of sighs'; 'in the little vault'; 'when the panting stops'; 'it must be nearly ended'. The effect is something like poetry, but it is far from being easily comprehensible. As we read it we try to make sense of it by searching for sentences, or parts of sentences, or phrases within it. We try to restructure it into grammatical patterns instinctively.

James Joyce ended his experimental novel *Ulysses* (1922) with a famous monologue – a powerful flow of language that conveys the random thoughts and associations forming in the mind of his character Molly Bloom. In order to convey this powerful flow of Molly's thoughts Joyce also leaves out punctuation altogether. If you have a copy of *Ulysses* to hand read through a couple of pages of the monologue aloud to get a feel for the extraordinary rhythms. More recently, the African-American novelist, Terry McMillan, used passages of almost entirely unpunctuated stream-of-consciousness in her novel, *How Stella Got Her Groove Back* (first published 1996). Here is a passage from it. Try reading it aloud:

> It just feels like nothing is the way it used to be anymore and it's not that I'm on some nostalgic trip or anything but I just wonder if I'm feeling like this because I can't believe I'm really forty-fucking-two years old because people tell me all the time I don't look forty-two and to be honest I don't have any immediate plans of really acquiring the *look* if there is a way to look when you're forty-two and I certainly don't feel forty-two even though I don't know how I'm supposed to *feel* being forty-two and what I do know is that I'm not *angry* about being forty-two but it feels like I'm slowly but surely catching up to my mama because she was only forty-two when she died and I'm thinking how is this possible that I could ever be the same age as mama? I wonder if I could secretly be having a midlife crisis?

(McMillan 1997: 9)

This piece of prose comes to life when it is read aloud. In fact it is much easier to understand when it is read aloud as the rhythms and intonations of the prose give us clues about where units of meaning begin and end. It is almost as if sentences or parts of sentences emerge from the stream as we read.

Some differences between writing and speech

Writing and speech are two overlapping but different kinds of verbal communication. The grammar of speech is much more loosely constructed than the grammar of writing, and sentence boundaries are often very unclear. One sentence appears to seep into another and we repeat ourselves in speech much more often than we do in writing. When we speak we use many kinds of non-linguistic forms of communication such as gestures and facial expressions, and the language we use is made more expressive through pacing, intonation and rhythm. In speech half-sentences and contractions of words work in a way that they wouldn't in formal writing.

Here is a transcript of a television discussion between writers and literary critics discussing a new book by the American novelist Don DeLillo:

Salman Rushdie: I think *Underworld* is the novel of DeLillo's life. He's been working his way up to this novel through a number of wonderful books. I think it has a very good chance of surviving.

David Aaronovitch: Nigella, you lead a pretty busy life. Were you pleased that Salman had recommended an 827-page epic? (Laughter)

Nigella Lawson: Well, now you mention it, I have to say, Salman, I did think, do I need to read a book like this? And I also have to say that – this is an awful confession to make – I bought *Underworld* when it first came out and I took it home and I kept thinking I was going to read it. I knew I wanted to read it, but I didn't. But you know the minute I started I just felt immensely grateful. I was cross with myself for not having started it earlier, but I just thought that it was so wonderful. You talk about the scope, but I loved the mix between the intimate and the epic which I think is amazing. At the very beginning – the baseball scene – when I started reading it, it was like a panning shot in cinema and I thought, how interesting, he's taking on what film can do and really this is what you would have in a film. And then as you carry on you realise that what he's doing actually is much more than film can do and he's reminding us about why we need writing. I just thought it was amazing.

(*Booked*, A Diverse Production for Channel Four, December 1998)

Although this is a formal situation – four speakers are sitting in a studio with cameras on them – the discussion itself is deliberately informal. The producers want to make us feel that we are observers of a spontaneous conversation between literary specialists who know each other well. Nigella Lawson's contribution here, for instance, is speculative. She is not reading from a script; she is working out what she thinks as she goes along. The sentences are quite long and they are mainly made up of a number of groups of words joined together by 'and', 'but' or 'or', and there is a good deal of repetition and self-interruption. There are also a number of idiosyncrasies of speech which are peculiar to this speaker: Nigella Lawson often uses the phrase 'I just thought' or 'I just felt', for instance. All of this makes a transcriber's work difficult. He or she must find a way of staying true to the original looseness and fragmentation of spoken English whilst transcribing it into the more formal sentence constructions of written English.

ACTIVITY 1:

In the transcription of the discussion above, some of the fragmentary features of speech have been ironed out, like creases in a shirt. In the following passage they have all been left in:

A: I've been there too

B: yeah

C: did did you . . . I went twice you go an fill in this great big long um questionnaire . . . takes ages . . . About all about

B: ah yes

A: whether you're happy . . . often an things like that

C: where

B: you know . . . It's in George Street

C: oh yes . . . I get it

A: then you go back later an he . . . he gives you well he tells you all about your personality an things but I never went back so I don't know . . . can't um you know really say

B: I did actually

A: what did he tell you

C: what did he say

B: well I was very sceptical before I went I uh you know I think well I think its all rubbish actually . . . an I went just um some . . . friends said come along . . . an um they said well . . . this woman takes you by yourself and she says . . . she she has a graph this is your personality

A: um

B: your good points up there an an your bad points down here she . . . she goes through them all and she asks you is this right . . . an I just said yeah that's OK an she said now knowledge can bring up your bad points to above the line so that they're good points . . . so would you like to come back for a lecture and stuff

A: yes well I

B: I just said no

(By kind permission of Rob Pope)

Take half of the passage directly above and rewrite it to make it less fragmented and more like the first passage. What kinds of changes did you have to make in order to transpose it into grammatically complete sentences? What does this tell you about the differences between written and spoken language? Write a few sentences reflecting on the process of transposition.

The interplay between spoken and written language structures

We have looked at writing which is more like speech (the Joyce passage) and speech which is more like writing (the experts' discussion). It is best to think of an interplay between writing and speech, rather than a simple contrast. E-mail, somewhere between a telephone conversation and a letter, has evolved as a very informal and speech-based form of writing because electronic communication has reduced the time between our messages, making it much more like conversation. Some people write scripts for themselves or others to speak, for instance for newsreaders or programme presenters or lecturers. Some scripted speeches sound very written and some sound very spoken, depending on the context for which they are written. Therefore it is perhaps better to think about both speech and writing in relation to *genres*. How we write and speak and how we use grammar in our writing and speaking depends upon audience, context and the genre of our communication.

Everyone is familiar with the term 'genre' in literature, but genre can also be applied to everyday speaking and writing to describe the type of writing or communication we choose to use in a particular situation. We shift between different genres all day and every day in our different activities and we do so without thinking. Different genres of communication might include a contribution to a meeting or classroom discussion, a professional letter, a letter to a friend, a shopping list, an essay. The way you write and speak and the grammar you use to write or speak depends upon the genre you use.

Knowing language and knowing 'about' language

If you are able to read, write and speak you already intuitively know the grammatical conventions and structures on which sentences are built and are able to adapt them constantly to different uses. It is this knowledge that comes to the fore when you read a passage like that of Beckett or Joyce. Your desire to understand, to receive the communication that is offered to you, makes you try to process it through your understanding of grammatical structures. David Crystal in *The Encyclopaedia of the English Language* reminds us that as adult English language speakers and writers we have already acquired the following:

- a vocabulary of between 40,000 and 50,000 words and an ability to understand about half as many again
- at least a thousand aspects of grammatical construction, governing the patterns of sentence and word formation
- approximately 20 vowels and 24 consonants and over 300 ways of combining these sounds into other sounds
- hundreds of ways of manipulating the sounds of language to convey meaning through pitch, speed, intonation, tone, and rhythm
- knowledge of the vast number of ways that the English language differs according to gender, class, occupation and region, and the ability to understand (and even place or imitate) many different dialects and accents
- knowledge of a large number of ways in which the patterns and conventions that govern language structures can be bent or broken in order to achieve special effects such as jokes or poems.

(Crystal 1997: 426)

So you already know grammar. In fact you already know 'at least a thousand different aspects of grammatical construction' and you already manipulate the conventions of grammar use across a number of different genres of communication. As writers, you are guided, even if faintly and intuitively, by your own version of a particular variety, or genre, of writing; by a particular level or style of language; and by whom you think is going to read what you have written.

However, whilst your present knowledge of grammar began in infancy and will continue through your adult life, it is *implicit* knowledge. This means that you use it but, unless you have been taught grammar before, you will not be able to explain what you know – to yourself and others – because you will not have a vocabulary to describe it. In this book we aim to make your implicit knowledge *explicit*. The most practical way to develop explicit grammatical knowledge is by analysing some varieties of language in use – to which we now turn.

The grammar of sentences

A sentence, as we all know, is the territory that lies between a capital letter and a full stop, but this definition, although absolutely accurate, does not take us very far because the question remains: 'well, what kinds of things *do* lie between a capital letter and a full stop?' As a first step in exploring this territory, we would like you to read the following story we have written. We have tried to copy the formula used by the hundreds of colourful board-books produced for pre-school children:

> Little Teddy puts on his vest. Little Teddy puts on his trousers. Little Teddy puts on his jumper. Little Teddy puts on his shoes. Little Teddy is tired. Little Teddy goes to sleep.

The story is simple and, without engaging pictures, perhaps rather dull. But it achieves a good deal for the number of words it uses, telling the narrative of Little Teddy's morning routine in six sentences, each describing a different stage in a larger process. What can we say about the kinds of sentences used in this story and the hundreds of published books like it? Without a vocabulary of grammatical terms what we can say is limited: they are all short and they are all very similar. Later in the book we will show you in much more detail how they are similar – in grammatical terms. For the moment we will point out that each of the sentences begins with 'Little Teddy' and then tells us what he is doing. In some sentences he is doing something to something else – putting on his shoes, or putting on his vest. But they all follow a similar pattern. It is a very repetitive piece of writing and uses a limited vocabulary.

This short narrative is written for a small child of about two years old who has a basic vocabulary, an ability to follow simple sentences, has grasped the fact of narrative progression, but probably has a limited attention span. The sentences are designed to work with pictures so that the child widens his or her vocabulary by hearing the word 'shoes' as he or she sees Teddy putting on his shoes. There is almost always a great deal of repetition in children's books, which enables the child to memorise new words and constructions. Rhythmic patternings and rhyming songs and nursery rhymes also help children to memorise new words and phrases. If you have read children's books to young children, you will know that the adult experience of reading such books aloud varies enormously. Some books are repetitive in mind-numbingly irritating ways, whereas others have an incantatory and even poetic quality which makes them a pleasure to read again and again.

Children's books for the under-fives generally:

- work within a limited vocabulary range
- use a high degree of repetition
- are short because the child's attention span is limited
- use very simple sentences
- use simple tenses.

A great deal can be achieved by skilled writers working within these constraints.

ACTIVITY 2:

Imagine you are the author of 'Little Teddy'. The book has been so successful that the publisher has decided to commission a series and has asked you to produce three more adventures or days in the life of Little Teddy. Write three more short narratives for Little Teddy of about the same length using more or less the same sentence structures as the original. Now write a short commentary identifying the limitations of writing in this way. In what kinds of writing would these limitations cause the greatest difficulties?

The grammar of children's stories

In 1963 Maurice Sendak wrote a classic story for children called *Where the Wild Things Are* about a mischievous little boy called Max who is sent to bed without his supper. In his room the angry boy witnesses all sorts of weird and wonderful things: a forest grows and a boat comes to fetch him and he sails to the land of the wild things and the wild things make him king and they all have a 'wild rumpus' until Max feels sad and wants to come home and he sails back home to his own room where he finds his supper waiting for him. I have summarised the story in this way in order to mimic the way it is written, which is primarily through long sentences made up of short clauses joined by 'and'. Here is part of the third sentence in the story as an illustration of Sendak's method of writing or 'prose style':

> And when he came to the place where the wild things are they roared their terrible roars and gnashed their terrible teeth and rolled their terrible eyes and showed their terrible claws

(Sendak 1963: 17–18)

What makes this story so famously successful with children and the adults who enjoy reading it to them? If you have the book to hand, read through it, paying particular attention to the length of the sentences and the way in which these long sentences are extended over several pages so that you only see parts of them on each page alongside the extraordinary and beautiful illustrations. Read the sentences aloud to get a feel of their rhythms.

If we were considering the story's success solely in relation to its literary content we might say that *Where the Wild Things Are* offers a highly imaginative interpretation of a child's mind when awake and asleep. It explores the child's experience of anger by turning that experience into a narrative of a journey to another land followed reassuringly by a return to the mother and home which are represented as stable and consistent. It explores cycles of power and authority in the way that Max talks to the monsters as his mother talks to him. And finally we might comment on the way that time is handled in the story. As Max disappears into his anger, time expands and contracts in strange dreamlike ways, and Sendak describes time as if it were a physical place.

But what might we say about *how* it was written and the vocabulary and forms of sentences that Sendak uses and how these contribute towards the effect of the story? What can we say about its form? Without detailed knowledge of grammatical structures we might begin by saying that Sendak uses much longer and more varied sentences than, say, 'Little Teddy'. We might comment on the way in which the language has powerful rhythms and even on the vividness of the vocabulary in the piece. We could get this far in our analysis without any knowledge of sentence grammar. But if we were interested in finding out how Sendak puts these extraordinary sentences together to make these strong rhythms, we would begin to need more explicit knowledge of sentence types and sentence construction.

A basic perception about sentences is that they are 'short' or 'long', but these words are, of course, so vague and elastic. How long is long? A further and more useful perception is that some sentences are easy to follow, others are hard to follow and perhaps need to be read twice. Long sentences are often the trickiest to understand. Sendak's story, like most stories, is made up of a mixture of sentences of different lengths. All of his long sentences, however, are perfectly easy to follow as of course they have to be for a children's story. How does he achieve this easy reading?

ACTIVITY 3:

- Read the section of the Sendak sentence we have given you above. Now break up this long sentence into as many shorter ones as you can by taking out the 'and's and putting in full stops where you can. You may have to adjust the wording a little. Then check the sequence of sentences makes sense. How many sentences do you have now?
- If you have access to an original copy of the book, look at the way Sendak, who is also the illustrator, has split the sentences up, giving some segments a page to themselves. Does this layout change the way we read the book? Does it change the way we read the individual sentences? Write up your answers as a short commentary.

The *and/but/or* family: the first group of connectives

Sendak's sentences in *Where the Wild Things Are* are easy to follow because they are predominantly made up of a series of 'mini-sentences' joined by the word 'and'. These 'mini-sentences' are called *clauses* and in the next chapter we will tell you about them in more detail. If you join a series of clauses with the word 'and', you are putting units of meaning together one after the other in a chain, end to end, in a way that is easy follow: 'this happened *and* then this happened *and* then he said . . .'. The word 'and', then, has a very significant *connective* function. 'And' is not the only connective of this kind. It is part of a small 'family' of words which have the same function in sentence construction. These are the words:

> and   but   or

They are called *conjunctions* or *connectives*. We have two terms to describe them because one expresses the class or form of the words and the other expresses the function. The term 'conjunction' classifies: it tells us about the word class (like 'nouns' or 'verbs') to which these words belong – they are 'conjunctions'. The word 'connective' on the other hand is used to describe the work that the words do, or the functions.

> Form: conjunction
> Function: connective

It is important to be aware that all words, all language in fact, can be analysed into *form* and *function*, as we shall stress throughout this book.

Notice two further features of the word 'and'. It can join clauses but it can also join single words, for example:

> night   *and*   day

and also phrases, for example:

> through the car park   *and*   between the gates   *and*   alongside the main entrance

The word 'and' is also used at the beginning of sentences in *Where the Wild Things Are*, which is unusual in most formal writing but is a stylistic feature of writing for children and of allegorical writing as we will see later in this chapter.

Co-ordinate clauses

We have said that *and/but/or* join clauses in a chain, end to end. This means that such clauses are all essentially *independent* of each other and therefore one is not more significant or dominant than another. Another way of describing it is that a sentence made up of clauses joined by *and/but/or* is like a series of railway carriages shackled together. They are, we can say, grammatically equal and potentially free-standing. The grammatical term for this relationship of equality between independent (or potentially independent) clauses is *co-ordinate*. In this context it means 'of the same order or status'. So we could say that Sendak's *Where the Wild Things Are* has a heavily co-ordinated sentence style. Maurice Sendak writes this way in order to achieve certain effects that are appropriate to a child's imagination and way of telling stories, but this heavily co-ordinated sentence style can be very effective in writing for adults too. Here are two examples of a co-ordinated style used to achieve different effects. The first is from a short story by the South-African writer Olive Schreiner (1855–1920) whose most famous novel, *Story of an African Farm*, was published in 1883. This passage is from a short story she wrote called 'Three Dreams in a Desert' which we might call a feminist parable or allegory. It was read by many suffragettes in the last decades of the nineteenth century. It is a story of liberation. The style she uses draws on ancient oral story-telling forms and incorporates biblical language and rhythms in its repeated use of co-ordinated clauses joined by strings of 'ands'. Unlike Sendak, however, Schreiner prefers shorter sentences, so she begins many of her sentences with 'And'. Her parable echoes the famous and very influential seventeenth-century allegory by John Bunyan, *The Pilgrim's Progress*, which also takes the form of a dream narrative. Compare the following passages below, the first from Schreiner's late nineteenth-century 'Three Dreams in a Desert' and the second passage which is the opening to Bunyan's seventeenth-century *Pilgrim's Progress*:

> I thought I stood on the border of a great desert, and the sand blew about everywhere. And I thought I saw two great figures like beasts of burden of the desert, and one lay upon the sand with its neck stretched out, and one stood by it. And I looked curiously at the one that lay upon the ground, for it had a great burden on its back, and the sand was thick about it, so that it seemed to have piled over it for centuries.
>
> And I looked very curiously at it. And there stood one beside me watching. And I said to him, 'What is this huge creature who lies here on the sand?'
>
> And he said, 'This is woman; she that bears men in her body.'
>
> (Schreiner in Showalter 1993: 309)

As I walked through the wilderness of this world, I lighted on a certain place where was a Den, and I laid me down in that place to sleep: and, as I slept, I dreamed a dream. I dreamed, and behold, I saw a man clothed with rags, standing in a certain place, with his face from his own house, a book in his hand, and a great burden upon his back. I looked, and saw him open the book, and read therein; and, as he read, he wept, and trembled; and, not being able longer to contain, he brake out with a lamentable cry, saying, What shall I do?

(Bunyan n.d.: 17)

If Schreiner was influenced by Bunyan, Bunyan was in his turn influenced by the powerful language and rhythms of the *King James Bible* (translated 1611) in writing the sentences of *The Pilgrim's Progress.* Compare the passage above from Bunyan's *Pilgrim's Progress* with the following passage from *Genesis* 9, for instance and you will see that whilst Bunyan, Sendak, Schreiner and the translators of the *King James Bible* all use strongly co-ordinated sentence styles to create a strong sense of narrative flow and rhythm, there are still interesting variations in the ways in which they use this heavily co-ordinated style:

And God spake until Noah, saying, Go forth of the ark, thou, and thy wife, and thy sons, and thy sons' wives with thee.

Bring forth with thee every living thing that is with thee, of all flesh, both of fowl, and of cattle, and of every creeping thing that creepeth upon the earth; that they may breed abundantly in the earth, and be fruitful, and multiply upon the earth.

And Noah went forth, and his sons, and his wife, and his sons' wives with him:

Every beast, every creeping thing, and every fowl, and whatsoever creepeth upon the earth, after their kinds, went forth out of the ark.

And Noah builded an altar unto the Lord; and took of every beast; and of every clean fowl, and offered burnt offerings on the alter.

(*King James Bible*, Genesis ch. 9, vs 15–19)

The *so/until/where* family: the second group of connectives

In our analysis of the grammatical structure and style of passages from *Genesis* to Maurice Sendak's *Where the Wild Things Are*, we have shown how useful it is to be aware of the connective work that the modest little word 'and' (and its siblings) achieves. But you may have wondered why we have only directed your attention to clauses joined by the 'and' family and have ignored clauses joined in other ways. It is now time to focus on the different kinds of connection that a much larger group of conjunctions – which includes 'so', 'until' and 'where' – makes between clauses. Consider, for example, the connection between these two clauses:

Schreiner's work became more allegorical after she had read Bunyan's *Pilgrim's Progress*.

These two clauses are joined not by *and/but/or* but by *after*. Of course, the two parts of the sentence can be reversed and still make sense:

After she had read Bunyan's *Pilgrim's Progress*, Schreiner's work became more allegorical.

Look again at the first version of the sentence above. What makes the relationship between the first clause and the second clause *different* from clauses joined by 'and', 'but' and 'or'? There are several points to consider here and they all hinge on the grammatical fact that *the second clause is not potentially independent but the first is*. You can test this by asking yourself if either of the clauses can stand alone and make complete sense. Would you agree that the first is complete on its own?

Schreiner's work became more allegorical.

But the second is *not* complete on its own:

After she had read Bunyan's *Pilgrim's Progress*.

The second clause, on its own, feels incomplete as though it needs to be linked up to another clause to complete its meaning. Also, the relationship between the two clauses is not equal or co-ordinate; the second *depends* upon the first. Think too of the meaning of the word 'after'. It tells you about an action; it tells you when it has happened. This complex relationship between the clauses is not something that the humble word 'and' could achieve.

We should, however, note that in speech 'and' is frequently used even when the implied connective meaning between clauses is more complex:

I got very cross *and* she left the room *and* she was furious with me.

In writing, the conjunctions in this sentence would probably be more precisely chosen:

I got very cross *so* she left the room *because* she was furious with me.

Here is another example of two clauses in which one is dependent upon the other:

> Sarah said she would be away during March so we didn't send her an invitation.

The first word of the second clause (the conjunction 'so') tells us that Sarah wasn't sent an invitation as a 'result' or 'consequence' of her being away in March. Again, the first clause could stand alone whereas normally the second could not. Try saying these clauses out aloud to see if you agree.

Co-ordinating conjunctions and co-ordinate clauses

Some people may find the term 'co-ordinating conjunction' appealing but we must admit we find it rather heavy and lacking in charm! Nevertheless, it is the established term and you can see what it means: if you use 'and', 'but' and 'or' to join two or more clauses which could stand on their own and make completed sense then what you are doing is co-ordinating these clauses. The term co-ordinating conjunction describes the form of the word; the function of the word is described by the word 'co-ordinator' or 'connective'.

Subordinating conjunctions and subordinate clauses

'Subordinate' is quite a well-chosen word for those clauses which depend on other clauses to complete their meaning and are introduced by the second family of conjunctions called subordinating conjunctions. It does not mean 'inferior' exactly, but more the idea of being dependent on another unit. What are we going to call the other unit? If you wanted to be really technical, you could call it 'super-ordinate' because 'super-' means 'higher' and 'sub-' means 'lower'. However, most people are happier with the term 'main clause'. It is an important part of language awareness to be able to identify *main clauses* (independent) and *subordinate clauses* (dependent) in sentences because if a sentence is long and complex, being able to find the main clause(s) will help you to make sense of the whole sentence. We put this statement in the plural because the numbers of clauses can vary. You have to have at least one main clause but you can have more; you can have one or more subordinate clauses too. The following sentence has a main clause and a subordinate clause. Note that the main clause must be able to stand on its own. It must be able to be potentially independent.

> *When* I see you next week   we can discuss our holiday plans.

You should be able to see that the second clause is independent and is therefore the main clause. The first clause is dependent upon the main clause. It can also work the other way round if you change the structure of the sentence:

> We can discuss our holiday plans *when* I see you next week.

ACTIVITY 4:

The following sentence has three subordinate clauses (dependent) and two main clauses (independent); again identify which is which, labelling each one:

> *If* you go to the library *when* you need a book, the librarian will talk to you *and* he or she will show you around *so* that you do not get lost.

More about the large family of subordinating conjunctions

There are over forty subordinating conjunctions. We've laid some of them out here in the form of a table, adapted from a similar one in David Crystal's *Rediscover Grammar*:

Subordinating conjunctions	Examples	Meanings they express
After, as, before, since, till, until, when, while	I rang *while* you were out.	Time
Where, wherever	I'll see *where* he is.	Place
If, unless, in case, as long as, supposing	I'll go *if* you come with me.	Condition
Whereas, whilst, while	I can dance, *whereas* you can't.	Contrast
Except, but that, save that, excepting that	I'd go, *except* that I don't have the time.	Exception
Because, since, for	I can't go, *because* it's expensive.	Reason
To, in order to, so as to	I left early, *in order to* pick up my children.	Purpose
So, so that	She was hungry, *so* she ordered a pizza.	Result
As, like	Do *as* I say.	Similarity
As if, as though, like	It looks *as if* he's in.	Comparison
the . . . the	*The* more I do, *the* less I like it.	Proportion
Rather than, sooner than	I'd walk *rather than* go on a horse.	Preference

(From Crystal 1996: 205)

As you can see, some are one-word conjunctions:

so, until, where, when, if, after, since, while, unless, although, because

but there are a large number of two-word and three-word conjunctions such as:

as long as, even if, in order to, so that, even though

Independent and dependent clauses

There are four fundamental ways of constructing sentences out of clauses and being able to distinguish between dependent and independent clauses makes it much easier to tell the differences between the four different ways. Up to this point in this chapter, we have given you all the forms and functions of sentence grammar that you need in order to appreciate what these four ways are. Before we define and illustrate each one, we want to explore a little further what we have been saying about the fact that some clauses are independent in meaning and some are dependent.

There are, in fact, several kinds of dependent clause and when we come to describe them at the end of Chapter 2 we will be focusing on the different forms that mark them out. By contrast, there is only one kind of independent clause: its function is to make a completed meaning in itself. It will not contain words that make it subordinate in any way, of course.

So the idea that some clauses are dependent and some are independent goes right to the heart of sentence construction. One way in which awareness of this can be useful is when we turn our attention in Chapter 5 to punctuation, especially punctuation in essay writing, because the trickiest elements of punctuation become child's play if you remember *the principle of dependency and independency of clauses.*

ACTIVITY 5:

Each of the following sentences is made up of a main clause (independent) and at least one subordinate (dependent) clause. Put a circle around the main clause in each sentence:

When they first met, they felt the ease and comfort of old friends.
He missed the boat, even though he had arrived at the terminal in good time.
I had no friends until you came to live here.
When I first heard the fire-alarm, I hadn't smelled the smoke because I was in the darkroom.
Until she was in her late seventies, she wore dark glasses, platform shoes and purple silk every day.

The four kinds of sentence construction

We can now go on to describe the four forms of sentences in terms of clause construction.

The single-clause sentence

This will of course be an independent clause. They can, for example, make particularly dramatic moments in a story stand out. Such sentences are often called *simple sentences* in grammar books but this is a potentially confusing term. It does not necessarily mean simple in meaning but only simple in structure, consisting 'simply' of one clause. 'Hilary's disenchantment has intensified', for example, is not exactly simple in meaning but it is technically simple in form as it consists of one, independent clause. Single-clause sentences can be very short:

I love you.

but not always:

This stupendous fragmentariness heightened the dreamlike strangeness of her bridal life.

(Eliot 1965: 224)

The co-ordinate sentence

A co-ordinate sentence is a sentence made up of two or more independent clauses joined by *and/but/or* (or punctuated by a semi-colon – see Chapter 5). It is essentially a sentence in which all the clauses are main clauses because they are all on an equal footing grammatically. For example:

I have been to Switzerland *and* I have walked in the Alps *but* I have never climbed the Matterhorn.

All of these clauses could, if the writing you were doing required it, stand on their own and make one-clause sentences. This kind of sentence construction is sometimes called *compound* in grammar books. We will use the term *co-ordinate* in this book.

The sentence with one main clause plus one or more subordinate clauses

This is a common construction in many kinds of writing and is sometimes called a *complex* sentence. Here are some examples of the simplest kind, made up of a main (independent) clause and only *one* subordinate (dependent) clause (we've marked main clauses with an M and dependent clauses with a D):

> When the rain stopped, (D)   the sun shone. (M)
> We could not play that day (M)   because it was raining. (D)
> While he is in charge, (D)   I am not going to co-operate. (M)
> I went to the door (M)   after I heard the bell. (D)

Here are some examples of sentences made up of one main clause (independent) and *more than one* subordinate (dependent) clause:

> When the rain stopped, (D)   the rain shone (M)   until the wind changed direction again. (D)
> While he is in charge, (D)   I am not going to co-operate, (M)   unless he apologises. (D)
> We could not play that day (M)   because it was raining (D)   when the team arrived. (D)

Notice that:

- in all these sentences the subordinate and the main clauses are reversible without a change of meaning
- if a subordinate clause comes before the main clause, it is customary to put a comma between the clauses (we will go into this in more detail in Chapter 5)
- it is best to think of the subordinating conjunctions as part of the subordinate clauses as this is the word class which makes the clause subordinate.

The sentence made up of different numbers of co-ordinated main clauses plus one or more subordinate clauses

A long sentence would have to have at least one main clause to act as the foundation or anchor clause. But a sentence might well have two main clauses co-ordinated by *and/but/or* and two, three or more subordinate clauses. Also, these clauses could be in any order, as long as they made sense. Once again this is a common kind of sentence construction and is sometimes called *compound-complex* because it is a mixture of co-ordinate and subordinate clauses.

You can begin to see how an awareness of the basic clause composition of sentences can be useful in checking to see if sentences are well-formed or not, if they are accurately punctuated, if they make full, clear sense, and how the subordinate clauses relate to the main clause and contribute to its meaning. The following sentence from Schreiner's 'Three Dreams in a Desert' which we looked at earlier is a very good example of the flexibility and fluidity that can be achieved in a multiple-clause sentence:

> And I looked curiously at the one that lay upon the ground, for it had a great burden on its back, and the sand was thick about it, so that it seemed to have piled over it for centuries.
>
> (Schreiner in Showalter 1993: 309)

It consists of four clauses which we have set out in a table format.

Main clause	Subordinate clause
And I looked curiously at the one that lay upon the ground	*for* it had a great burden on its back,
and the sand was thick about it,	*so* that it seemed to have piled over it for centuries.

ACTIVITY 6:

We have set out the four different ways of constructing sentences as:

1. Simple	Single-clause sentence	e.g. Tennyson was appointed Poet Laureate in 1850.
2. Co-ordinate	Sentences made up of co-ordinated clauses (joined by and/but/or)	e.g. Tennyson published *In Memoriam* and was appointed Poet Laureate in 1850.
3. Subordinate	The sentence with one main clause plus one or more subordinate clauses	e.g. Tennyson held the position of Poet Laureate until he died in 1892.
4. Mixture of subordinate and co-ordinate	The sentence made up of several co-ordinated main clauses plus one or more subordinate clauses	Tennyson published *In Memoriam* and he was also appointed Poet Laureate in 1850 when Wordsworth died.

Write a short children's story using sentence structures 1, 2, 3, 4, 1, 2, 3, 4 etc. in that order. Experiment with sentence structures 3 and 4 as these can be very varied by arranging co-ordinate and subordinate clauses in different ways. Write a short commentary on your story and the effect this rather unusual patterning of sentence constructions creates.

Language in use: the functions of co-ordination and subordination

It is important to remember when studying grammar to think about it in relation to the purposes for which it is being *used*. Writers choose sentence forms for particular reasons – to suit a kind of writing or to suit a particular audience. Sendak, for instance, uses a heavily co-ordinated sentence style. Why does he do this? An answer might go something like the following:

> Sendak uses a predominantly co-ordinated style to create an urgently forward-moving rhythm in this story which reflects the strong energies and emotions of a child. Sendak tells us that Max sailed 'in and out of weeks and almost over a year' and this play with time and with pacing (everything seems to happen all at once) is mirrored in the fluidity of the sentences in which everything seems to flow into everything else creating a sense of inevitability. The co-ordinated style is also peculiar to children's speech, particularly when they are telling stories; they might say for instance: 'This morning I went to school and I saw my friend Peter and he said that his mum had given him a present and he showed me it'. 'And' co-ordination is also much used in oral narratives for adults as well as for children from the poetry of Robert Browning and the journalistic short stories of Dorothy Richardson to the prose of Garrison Keillor.

Sentences appear in hundreds of different shapes and sizes: from the simplest one-clause sentence:

> I love you.

to the most complex sentence of the novelist Henry James. Here is the opening sentence to his famous ghost story of 1898, *The Turn of the Screw*:

> The story held us, round the fire, sufficiently breathless, but except the obvious remark that it was gruesome, as on Christmas Eve in an old house a strange tale should essentially be, I remember no comment uttered till somebody happened to note it as the only case he had met in which such a visitation had fallen on a child.

(James 1981: 3)

Writers do not sit down and think 'I shall begin with a heavily subordinated sentence and finish up with a single-clause sentence as a climax', but rather they write sentences in order to achieve particular effects. The powerful 'I love you' is a direct and passionate statement. It works because it is not qualified or conditional or wrapped up in other complex statements that take away its simple power such as:

> I would like to say that I love you, but to be honest it is only possible to say that I love you when you are kind to me and when you are not always having a go at me.

Henry James's style is world-famous for being complex and intricate and often difficult to follow. In *The Turn of the Screw* the story itself is as intricate and twisting as his first sentence, quoted above. If he had written a simpler version of the sentence instead, such as 'The story was so gripping that nobody spoke', a huge amount of important information would be lost: that it was Christmas, that it was being told by one person to a group of others in an old house in front of a fire, that it was gruesome and involved something terrible happening to a child. Henry James is a master of suspense and suggestion because he can pack all these things into one sentence casually and suggest that all these things are somehow interconnected. In order to achieve this suspense he uses a heavily subordinated style with a manipulation of sentence construction so that the main clauses of the sentence 'the story held us round the fire sufficiently breathless . . . I remember no comment uttered' are actually no more important than all the subsidiary information.

However, complex sentences of the kind that Henry James uses so masterfully on the printed page in a ghost story can in other situations be a positive obstacle to communication. Edith Wharton, a novelist and friend of Henry James, described going on a shopping expedition with James, to London's King's Road. When the two lost their way, James decided to ask a taxi driver for directions:

> 'My friend, to put it to you in two words, this lady and I have just arrived here from *Slough*; that is to say, to be more strictly accurate, we have recently *passed through* Slough on our way here, having actually motored to Windsor from Rye, which was our point of departure; and the darkness having overtaken us, we should be much obliged if you would tell us where we are now in relation, say, to the High Street, which, as you of course know, leads to the Castle, after having on the left hand the turn down to the railway station.'
>
> I was not surprised to have this extraordinary appeal met by silence, and a dazed expression on the old wrinkled face at the window; nor to have James go on: 'In short' (his invariable prelude to a fresh series of explanatory ramifications), 'in short, my good man, what I want to put to

you in a word is this: supposing we have already (as I have reason to think we have) driven past the turn down to the railway station (which, in that case, by the way, would probably not have been on our left hand, but on our right), where are we now in relation to . . .'

'Oh, please', I interrupted, feeling myself utterly unable to sit through another parenthesis, 'do ask him where the King's Road is.'

'Ah–? The King's Road? Just so! Quite right! Can you, as a matter of fact, my good man, tell us where in relation to our present position the King's Road exactly *is*?'

'Ye're in it,' said the aged face at the window.

(Leavis 1983: 184–5)

ACTIVITY 7:

Here are two sentences in which subordinate clauses predominate. The first is a made-up sentence:

> Because I have never been to Switzerland or walked in the Alps, I am determined to stay in Zurich this summer, even though it will be expensive.

Identify the main clause in the above sentence. Identify the remaining clauses. Transpose the whole sentence into co-ordinated clauses (you will need to adapt the wording slightly to do this). Compare the new sentence to the original. Which do you prefer and why?

The second heavily subordinated sentence is taken from David Crystal's *Rediscover Grammar* (1996). It is the first sentence of a short paragraph. Identify the main clause in this first sentence.

> If we read the newspapers or listen to newscasters around the English-speaking world, we will quickly develop the impression that there is a World Standard English (WSE), acting as a strongly unifying force among the vast range of variation which exists. However, this impression is not entirely correct. A totally uniform, regionally neutral, and arguably prestigious variety does not yet exist worldwide.

(Crystal 1996: 14)

Sentence types and communication

In the preceding sections we have been exploring and analysing the four different kinds of sentence construction. This is not the same as what we mean by 'sentence types'. You should note the distinction between sentence *construction* and sentence *types*. Sentence types are the different kinds of communication that sentences produce and this is really quite simple.

Sentence type	Example
Declaratives (declare or state something)	I like you.
Interrogatives (ask something)	Do you like me?
Imperatives (command or request something)	Open the window.
Exclamatives (express with emphasis)	What a terrible noise you are making!

By far the most common sentence type used in writing is the declarative or statement-making type. The picture is much more mixed in spoken language.

In this chapter we have been looking at sentence grammar. Later in the book we will look at word grammar, phrase grammar and finally text grammar. But we haven't finished with sentence grammar yet. There are important further features of sentence grammar to be analysed but these will be considered in the next chapter. For the time being, we would like you to consolidate your implicit and explicit knowledge of the kinds of sentence construction we have looked at in this chapter by undertaking the following activities.

ACTIVITY 8:

Explore the use of sentence grammar in the following children's story, called *'The Story'*, written by Arnold Lobel and published in 1970.

- Find examples of co-ordinate clauses.
- Find examples of subordinate clauses.
- Note the presence of both narrative repetition and grammatical repetition – what does this contribute to the effect of the story?

One day in summer Frog was not feeling well. Toad said, 'Frog, you are looking quite green.' 'But I always look green,' said Frog. 'I am a frog.' 'Today you look very green even for a frog,' said Toad. 'Get into my bed and rest.'

Toad made Frog a cup of hot tea. Frog drank the tea, and then he said, 'Tell me a story while I am resting.' 'All right,' said Toad. 'Let me think of a story to tell you.' Toad thought and thought. But he could not think of a story to tell Frog.

'I will go out on the front porch and walk up and down,' said Toad. 'Perhaps that will help me to think of a story.' Toad walked up and down on the porch for a long time. But he could not think of a story to tell Frog.

Then Toad went into the house and stood on his head. 'Why are you standing on your head?' asked Frog. 'I hope that if I stand on my head, it will help me to think of a story,' said Toad. Toad stood on his head for a long time. But he could not think of a story to tell Frog.

Then Toad poured a glass of water over his head. 'Why are you pouring water over your head?' asked Frog. 'I hope that if I pour water over my head, it will help me to think of a story,' said Toad. Toad poured many glasses of water over his head. But he could not think of a story to tell Frog.

Then Toad began to bang his head against the wall. 'Why are you banging your head against the wall?' asked Frog. 'I hope that if I bang my head against the wall hard enough, it will help me to think of a story', said Toad.

'I am feeling much better now, Toad,' said Frog. 'I do not think I need a story any more.' 'Then you get out of bed and let me get into it', said Toad, 'because now I feel terrible.' Frog said, 'Would you like me to tell you a story, Toad?' 'Yes,' said Toad, 'if you know one.'

'Once upon a time', said Frog, 'there were two good friends, a frog and a toad. The frog was not feeling well. He asked his friend the toad to tell him a story. The toad could not think of a story. He walked up and down on the porch, but he could not think of a story. He poured water over his head, but he could not think of a story. He banged his head against the wall, but he still could not think of a story. Then the toad did not feel so well, and the frog was better. So the toad went to bed and the frog got up and told him a story. The end. How was that, Toad?' said Frog.

But Toad did not answer. He had fallen asleep.

(Lobel 1970: 16–27)

ACTIVITY 9:

Write a parable for adults using a co-ordinated sentence style like that of Olive Schreiner or write a story for older children in imitation of the prose rhythms and co-ordinated sentence style of Maurice Sendak. Add a few sentences explaining what you were trying to do.

ACTIVITY 10:

Writing for children is not just about being imaginative: it depends a good deal on knowing how children acquire language and the different stages they reach along the way. Publishers who specialise in books for children will need to have a working knowledge of child language acquisition too.

You have just joined a publishing house which specialises in children's books. Your employer has asked you to give her a report on the text of 'Little Teddy', *Where the Wild Things Are* and 'The Story' in order to assess which age group each of the three stories is suitable for so that they can be properly placed in the publisher's catalogue. She has given you the following sheet from an introduction to child language development to help you assess them. Write a report of no more than 200 words for your employer.

Child language acquisition

On one level the acquisition of language and grammar is a gradual process but on another level it also happens very quickly. Children *understand* language before they begin to use it. The child usually utters her first word before she is one year old and these first words are usually labels or *nouns*: 'shoe', 'dog', 'food', or 'mummy' or 'daddy'. For a long time children just add to their store of labels, adding a few *verbs* along the way such as 'goes', 'eats', 'sleeps'. By the time they are about eighteen months old toddlers may have a store of 200 nouns.

Then the child begins to play with these words, preparing herself for the next stage. At this stage she learns the uses of intonation so that 'dog' may become 'dog?' or 'Dog!'. Soon after this comes the two-word stage, in which the child adds another word to the noun to communicate more. For instance she might say 'more ball' or 'John ball' or 'where Ted?'

From this point until they are about two years old, children begin to learn strictly communicative and logical patterns of grammar by adding simple verbs or adjectives to the store of nouns: 'see Jane' or 'naughty Jane'. These are primitive sentence structures – 'cat jump' (subject + verb) or 'shut door' (verb + object) – and show knowledge of English word order. Eventually tenses start to appear but in the early years they follow logical grammar rules, before they learn the huge number of exceptions to the grammatical tenses: hence children will say 'I comed' or 'Jane goed' until they learn to say 'I came' or 'Jane went' by listening and imitating.

The next step is learning to add words to these basic structures, to fill them out into fuller sentences. These first sentences are often a kind of telegraphese: 'see lots mans' rather than 'see what a lot of men'. Gradually the jerky uneven speech becomes more and more fluent as the child learns the exceptions to the grammar rules – e.g. 'I went' rather than 'I goed' – and acquires a greater vocabulary of adjectives, verbs and adverbs with which to communicate with more subtlety. By the age of three or four the child may have a vocabulary of about 500–600 different words but actually use 20,000 words in a single day. Repetition is an important part of the child's world.

At the age of about three, sentences become much longer as children learn to string their sentences together. The word 'and' is the key word at this stage: 'I did go to the shops and buy a cake and my mummy she did say that I could have the cake with the cherry on the top and I ate it all by myself'. Other common linking words at this stage are 'because', 'so', 'then', 'when', 'if' and 'before'.

At the age of about four, children begin to learn the hundreds of exceptions to the grammatical patterns and all the irregular verbs so that by school age the quaint little expressions ('I did go', 'I singed the song') that have characterised their earlier speech have all but disappeared. Throughout the school years the process continues so that the child's language structures become more and more varied and flexible through reading, speaking and early writing practice.

Summary

In this chapter we have introduced you to:

- grammar in speech and writing
- implicit and explicit knowledge of grammar
- sentence construction in writing for children
- co-ordinating conjunctions and subordinating conjunctions
- independent and dependent clauses
- the four ways of constructing sentences:
  - simple or one-clause sentences
  - sentences using co-ordination
  - sentences using subordination
  - sentences using both co-ordination and subordination
- sentence types: declarative, interrogative, imperative, exclamative
- the stages of child language acquisition.

References

Beckett, Samuel (1973) 'How It Is' in Hugh Kenner, *A Reader's Guide to Samuel Beckett*. London: Thames and Hudson.

Bunyan, John (n.d.) *The Pilgrim's Progress from this World to that which is to Come Delivered Under the Similitude of a Dream by John Bunyan*. London: The Religious Tract Society.

Crystal, David (1996) *Rediscover Grammar*. Harlow: Longman.

Crystal, David (1997) *The Encyclopaedia of the English Language* [1995]. Cambridge: Cambridge University Press.

Eliot, George (1965) *Middlemarch* [1871–72]. Harmondsworth: Penguin.

James, Henry (1981) *The Turn of the Screw* [1898]. London: Bantam Books.

Joyce, James (1960) *Ulysses* [1922]. London: The Bodley Head.

King James Bible, Cambridge: Cambridge University Press.

Leavis, F.R. (1983) *The Great Tradition* [1948]. Harmondsworth: Penguin.

Lobel, Arnold (1970) 'The Story' in *Frog and Toad are Friends*. London: Harper Collins Juvenile Books.

McMillan, Terry (1997) *How Stella Got Her Groove Back* [1996]. Harmondsworth: Penguin.

Sendak, Maurice (1963) *Where the Wild Things Are*. London: Penguin Books in association with The Bodley Head.

Showalter, Elaine (1993) *Daughters of Decadence: Women's Writing of the Fin-de-Siecle*. London: Virago.

The anatomy of the clause

Rebecca Stott and Peter Chapman

In a book like this we have to 'freeze-frame' language in action, as it flows along all around us, in order to look a bit more closely at what holds it together. Language structures are intricate and closely interconnected, and to understand one part you have to understand a little of how it all fits together. You could describe language as like a machine, or like a body, or like a community. It is an interconnected system which depends upon all its parts functioning in particular ways, as individuals and as a whole. There are limitations to all these metaphors, of course, but if we were to describe sentence grammar as like a body, in the last chapter we were dealing with the limbs and how they are joined, whereas in this chapter we look *inside* the limbs to see how they are constructed. In other words, we have looked at how clauses are related to each other and now we will look at the *internal* make-up of the clause. We have divided this chapter into two parts. First we will explain and illustrate the internal structure of clauses and then we will return to the contrast between independent and dependent clauses we developed in Chapter 1 and introduce you to a few more important kinds of dependent clause.

Sometimes students of literature complain that literary criticism, particularly the close examination of passages from literary texts, feels too much like a science. They even use scientific metaphors to complain that literary analysis of a certain kind is like 'dissecting' something or looking at it under a microscope. By this they mean that dissecting ruins not only the integrity and perfection of the poem under examination but also their pleasure in that poem. William Wordsworth described this view in a famous poem, 'The Tables Turned', when he said:

> Our meddling intellect
> Misshapes the beauteous forms of things; –
> We murder to dissect.

(ll. 25–8)

But you could argue it differently: that to see something very closely, as if through a microscope, is not to see a different object, but to see the same object from a different vantagepoint. The Victorians discovered the beauty of the microscopic when the microscope became affordable for many in the 1860s. At that time poets and novelists in particular described the fascination of seeing something already minute, such as a fly's wing or a human hair, magnified hundreds of times, because more than anything it made visible the extraordinary complexity and intricacy of anatomical structures. It was a kind of new world – or rather a series of worlds within worlds. Can the same be said of the grammatical study of language? That looking at it very closely will increase our appreciation of how beautiful and extraordinary language is? We hope so. At best the study of language can also stimulate wonder and awe. It need not be dull and narrowly technical.

The structure of clauses

In the last chapter we described clauses as 'mini-sentences' and we worked with the distinction between dependent and independent clauses; we relied on your intuitive grasp of whole clauses and we considered how clauses are related to each other. Now we can tell you that clauses are internally constructed from *a grammatical 'kit' of seven elements*, at least two of which are normally obligatory and the others optional. But before we go any further we want to explain exactly what we mean by 'a grammatical kit of seven elements'.

Clause elements: functions or forms?

Clauses can have a hugely varying number of words in them from a minimum of two to, well, twenty or more. The following one-clause sentence from Virginia Woolf's *Orlando* (1928), for example, has forty-six words:

And so, the thought of love would be ambered over with snow and winter; with log fires burning; with Russian women, gold swords, and the bark of stags; with old King James' slobbering and fireworks and sacks of treasure in the holds of Elizabethan sailing ships.

(Woolf 1993: 69)

This sentence has a 'subject' and a 'verb' (see below) and one other element repeated eight times. The subject of the sentence is 'the thought of love' and the verb is 'would be ambered over'. The rest of the sentence tells us precisely *how* the thought of love would be 'ambered over' (i.e. *with X, with Y, with Z*). ('Ambered' is a great word to use here. It is not usually used as a verb but Woolf is poetic in her use of language and here she is writing about how memory works to set clusters of diverse objects together just as diverse objects from a distant time can be found fossilized in amber. Hence 'the thought of love would be ambered over'.)

When we use the term 'element', then, to describe the parts of a clause, we mean its *functional parts not its individual words*. Now the idea that there may be up to seven different elements in a clause all serving different functions starts to look more interesting and useful to know. For example, in the sentence just quoted there are forty-six words but only three of the elements are present, one of them several times. We shall return to this example shortly. This means that any of the seven elements can be expressed by one word or several, as you will see.

In Chapter 3 we shall be focusing on word classes. If you find we use word-class terms (like 'noun' and 'verb') in this chapter in a way you find unclear, then you should jump forward to Chapter 3 for clarification or revision.

We will begin by giving you a table of all the seven elements with brief explanations and examples. We can then go into detail within the framework we have established. Look through the table carefully and return to it when you need to as you work your way through this chapter, noting also the abbreviated forms in the last column:

The seven functional elements of the clause		
Subject	The agent in the clause: who or what the clause is about (e.g. '*The large tortoiseshell cat* walked towards her')	S
Verb	The action, process or state in the clause (e.g. 'She *had been watching* that cat for some time')	V
Adverbial	Words or phrases that modify or give extra definition to the verb (e.g. 'She arrived *at tea-time*')	A
Direct object	The person (or thing) directly affected by the action of the verb (e.g. 'She gave *the large brown parcel* to the policeman')	Od
Indirect object	The person (or thing) that is the recipient of the action of the verb (e.g. 'She gave the large brown parcel *to the policeman*')	Oi
Subject complement	The part of a clause that gives definition to the subject (e.g. 'She seemed *very sad indeed*')	Cs
Object complement	The part of a clause that adds meaning to the direct object (e.g. 'She found the play *difficult to understand*')	Co

The essential components of the clause: the subject and verb

When language analysts compare English with other languages, they often call English an SVO language (Subject, Verb, Object) to mean that this is often the order and structure of the elements in a clause.

Subject	Verb	Object
I	hate	television.
The detective	had been watching	the house.

This is quite a useful guide but it should not be taken too literally because language structures are flexible and varied. Because English speakers tend unconsciously to expect the order of a clause to be SVO, playing around with the word order can either impede the understanding of the reader or listener, or create interesting effects, depending on the skill of the writer. Writers might change the SVO structure to create specific rhythmic effects or to alter the emphasis of a statement or make it more emphatic. For example:

Object	Subject	Verb
Television	I	hate.

Another problem with describing the English language as an SVO language is that it implies that every clause has to have a subject element, a verb element and an object element. Actually, the only absolutely *essential* parts of a clause are a subject and a verb, or to be more precise in our terminology:

> A CLAUSE MUST NORMALLY HAVE AT LEAST A SUBJECT ELEMENT AND A VERB ELEMENT.

Of course, a clause will often have a good deal more than this – elements which we have not identified yet – but *without a subject and a verb, groups of words cannot normally be considered to be a clause*. In other words the object element is not an essential part of the clause unless the verb has to have an object to complete its meaning. Some verbs do not require to be attached to a direct object and some do. Compare these two examples:

Subject	Verb
I	slept.
The man in the blue suit	was smoking.

Subject	Verb	Object
I	hate	television.
The man in the blue suit	stepped into	his Ferrari.

Verbs which do not require to be followed by a direct object ('I slept') are called *intransitive* and verbs which do require a direct object ('I hate') are called *transitive*. Transitive means 'carried over', so a verb 'carries over' to an object – or not, as the case may be. Many verbs can be *either* transitive or intransitive, depending on the meaning you want to express. For example:

Verb	Example of intransitive form	Example of transitive form
To smoke	He smoked.	He smoked long black cigars.
To write	He's writing.	He's writing a letter.
To grow	The forest grew and grew.	The forest grew new leaves.

And there are some verbs which are *only* transitive: 'hate', for instance, is an interesting example of a transitive verb. You could say simply 'I hate', but most people would wait for you to finish the sentence because usually we don't talk about hating in an abstract way but rather we say we hate something in particular. (There are interesting philosophical implications to all of this, of course.) What you need to remember here is that usually a clause needs a subject element and a verb element and *sometimes* it will have to have an object element (as well as other elements on our chart).

As we have said, it is probably true to say that the *subject comes before the verb in the majority of English sentences*. However, we are going to start by looking not at the subject function but at the verb function. The reason for this is that it is easier to identify a clause by finding the verb because all (or nearly all) clauses have to have one and because subject words do not always come first in a clause as we might expect. So we shall go straight to the verb function and verb forms.

Inside the clause: the verb element

The verb is the nerve centre or nucleus of the clause. It is where the action is. When you were at school you may have been told that a verb is a 'doing word'. But verbs can tell us about states as well as actions, so we will describe verbs here as words in clauses which express ideas of *process* (for instance the verb 'to absorb' tells us about a process rather than an action), *actions* (for instance the verb 'to strike' or 'to write') and *states* (for instance 'to know' or 'to seem').

A sentence may have a single-word verb or a cluster of words expressing the verb element. When a verb element is made up of several words it will usually be a main verb accompanied by up to three *auxiliary* (meaning 'helper') verbs.

Subject	Auxiliaries	Main verb
She	was	watching.
The nursing staff	will be	assisting.
He	did	help.
The security guard	should have been	watching.

There are two different kinds of auxiliary verb:

Primary verbs: (*be*, was, were, is) (*have*, has, had) (*do*, does)
Modal verbs: can, could, will, would, shall, should, may, might, must

Full verbs

A full verb is a verb whose meaning can be clearly and independently identified. There are thousands of these and the numbers grow as new verbs are added to dictionaries every year. A recent addition is the verb 'to surf', derived from the noun 'surf' meaning 'white, foamy water', which means both 'surfing on waves' and also 'surfing the internet'. The verb 'to download' is another recent addition, once again created by the computer revolution of the last few decades.

Primary verbs

There are just three primary verbs: *be, have* and *do*. These can be used in two ways:

- as though they were full verbs as in 'I *am* a taxi-driver'; 'I *have* a new computer'; 'I *do* the cooking'
- or as auxiliary verbs attached to full verbs as in: 'I *am going* to London tomorrow'; 'I *have read* all those books'; '*Does* your friend *want* a drink?'.

When primary verbs are used as auxiliaries in this way they make the verb more precise in terms of, for example, the time in which the action takes place. For instance, consider the difference between 'he watched' and 'he had been watching' or the difference between 'he will watch' and 'he will have been watching'.

Modal verbs

'Modal' mainly means 'expressing degrees of probability or obligation' so a modal verb conveys a range of judgements about events. They only function as auxiliary (or 'helper') verbs and they work to add to, or define, or focus the meaning of the full verb. There are nine modal verbs which can be added to the full verb to express either probability or obligation:

can, could, may, might, will, would, shall, should, must

Consider the difference in meaning between:

I *will* pay you back tomorrow.
I *may* pay you back tomorrow.
I *should* pay you back tomorrow.

The expression of modality is a major function of language and is foun not only in modal verbs but also in words like 'probably' and 'possibly' (adverbs).

To sum up all of this we can say that verbs are marked for time through tenses and through primary verbs and for degrees of probability and obligation through modal verbs. From this brief sketch you can appreciate the extensive power and richness of the work that verbs do in clauses. We shall deal with the ways in which verbs express time (past, present and future) in Chapter 3.

ACTIVITY 1:

Identify as many verbs as you can in the following passage from the Nigerian novelist Chinua Achebe's *Things Fall Apart* (originally published in 1958). Don't forget that each will be the 'nucleus' of a clause.

Ekwefi had suffered a good deal in her life. She had borne ten children and nine of them had died in infancy, usually before the age of three. As she buried one child after another her sorrow gave way to despair and then to grim resignation. The birth of her children, which should be a woman's crowning glory, became for Ekwefi mere physical agony devoid of promise. The naming ceremony after seven market weeks became an empty ritual. Her deepening despair found expression in the names she gave her children. One of them was a pathetic cry, Onwumbiko – 'Death, I implore you.' But Death took no notice; Onwumbiko died in his fifteenth month. The next child was a girl, Ozoemena – 'May it not happen again.' She died in her eleventh month, and two others after her. Ekwefi then became defiant and called her next child Onwuma – 'Death may please himself.' And he did.

(Achebe 1986: 54)

Look for examples of the following:

- single-word verbs
- full verbs with auxiliaries, either modal or primary
- whether the verbs are expressing actions, processes or states.

Finite and non-finite forms of verbs

Verbs can usually be further classified into two broad types based on one more difference of meaning they express: *finite* and *non-finite*. The finite forms are those which limit (fix or make 'finite') the verb to a particular person, number and tense. First we will explain what we mean by person, number and tense.

When linguists talk about verbs they often need to be able to distinguish between the different forms that verbs take in sentences. They use a system to do this:

	Singular	Plural
First person	I rest	We rest
Second person	You rest	You rest
Third person	She/he/it rests	They rest

This means that the clause 'she rests' is in 'third person singular' and the clause 'we rest' is in 'first person plural', for instance. Thus we can say that the verb in 'the teacher sneezed' is in 'third person singular' and in the past tense. 'Non-finite' means not limited in any of these three ways (person, number and tense).

ACTIVITY 2:

Here is a table which identifies the person, number and tense of a series of verb elements. We have filled in the first few rows. Complete the rest.

Subject and verb elements	Person	Number	Tense
They touched	third person	plural	past
I will touch	first person	singular	future
We touched	first person	plural	past
The woman touches			
They will touch			
I touched			
The women touch			

Finding finite verbs is straightforward enough: if the verb has a tense (in the past, present or future) and a subject ('John kicked'), the verb will be finite. So what is a non-finite verb? There are three non-finite verb forms. The first two you can recognise by the ending:

> –ing: John lost his ticket, *travelling* to the theatre.
> –ed: Beatrice collapsed, *exhausted* from the heat.

Notice that 'travelling' and 'exhausted' are only non-finite in these sentences. They could be made into finite forms by adding number, person and tense. For example:

> John lost his ticket when *he was travelling* to the theatre.
> Beatrice collapsed because *she was exhausted* by the heat.

On their own within a non-finite clause, however, 'travelling' and 'exhausted' are detached from person, number and tense. The following examples make this clear:

> *Reading my essay through,* I noticed a number of mistakes.
> *Finding everything on TV completely boring,* I decided to go for a walk.
> *Asked to come early,* I arrived at three.
> *Studied with care,* Shakespeare's *Henry V* reveals a critical attitude to war.

Note that the clauses in italic are all dependent clauses: they cannot stand alone in terms of meaning. This is what they would look like if you tried to make them complete sentences:

> Reading my essay through this morning.
> Finding everything on TV completely boring.
> Asked to come early.
> Studied with care.

The last type of non-finite form is the 'to' form, otherwise called *the infinitive*:

Infinitive form	Example of use in a sentence
To go	I wanted *to go*.
To see	He stretched up *to see*.

ACTIVITY 3:

Write a short poem using a series of non-finite clauses of all three types and ending with a finite clause. Here's one we wrote earlier.

> *Intent*
> Slipping through crowds,
> To find his way,
> Creeping through byways,
> Threatened by glances,
> Protected by anonymity,
> Ducking and diving,
> He stalks his prey.

ACTIVITY 4:

Here is a passage from a short story called 'The Things They Carried' by Tim O'Brien (1990), which uses a number of finite and non-finite verbs to convey a sense of the horrific relentlessness of the soldiers' actions.

- Identify all the finite verbs in the passage and all the non-finite verbs.
- Are there any examples of primary verbs used as full verbs?
- Are there any examples of modal verbs?
- We have suggested that O'Brien's use of non-finite verbs conveys a sense of 'relentlessness' about what the soldiers are doing. What else can be said about the way verbs are used in this passage?

They plodded along slowly, dumbly, leaning forward against the heat, unthinking, all blood and bone, simple grunts, soldiering with their legs, toiling up the hills and down into the paddies and across the rivers and up again and down, just humping, one step and then the next and then another, but no volition, no will, because it was automatic, it was anatomy, and the war was entirely a matter of posture and carriage, the hump was everything, a kind of inertia, a kind of emptiness, a dullness of desire and intellect and conscience and hope and human sensibility. Their principles were on their feet. Their calculations were biological. They had no sense of strategy or mission. They searched the villages without knowing what to look for, not caring, kicking over jars of rice, frisking children and old men, blowing tunnels, sometimes setting fires and sometimes not, then forming up and moving on to the next village, then other villages, where it would always be the same.

(O'Brien 1990: 72)

Verbs in the passive voice

Consider these two sentences:

The boy carried the cat.
The cat was carried by the boy.

This difference is referred to as *voice*. The first sentence construction is described as being in the active voice and is much more common. It is called active because the subject of the sentence 'the boy' is active – he carried the cat. The second sentence construction is described as being in the passive voice. What has happened to these two sentences in grammatical terms? The subject and object have swapped places and have assumed different grammatical functions. In the second sentence the boy is now the *passive agent* ('by the boy') and the object ('the cat'), now moved to the front of the sentence, is the *passive subject*.

Here is another example:

> He was sent to bed.

The combination of 'was' and 'sent' tells us that this verb is in the passive voice (e.g. 'was sent', 'was driven', 'was ordered', 'was paid'). Passive verbs can, of course, be in any tense: for example, 'he will be sent' and 'he is being sent' are just as common. In this sentence the boy 'was sent'. He is the passive subject of the sending. The agent of the sending (presumably the boy's mother) is not actually mentioned in this sentence. The writer might have included her by writing 'the boy was sent to bed by his mother', but presumably he has decided that what is important is that the boy 'was sent' to bed. The action is more important to the writer perhaps than the person who did the sending.

Here are some more examples of verbs in the passive voice. What they have in common is that the verb has a passive subject. Some have agents included and some don't. As you can see, the form the passive takes depends upon the tense of the verb being used:

Active voice	Passive voice with agent	Passive voice without agent
The government has raised taxes.	Taxes *have been raised* by the government.	Taxes *have been raised*.
My grandfather planted the tree.	The tree *was planted* by my grandfather.	The tree *was planted*.
You should have shut these doors.	These doors *should have been shut* by you.	These doors *should have been shut*.
They broke the window.	The window *was broken* by them.	The window *was broken*.
We keep the eggs in there.	The eggs *are kept* in there by us.	The eggs are kept in there.
I weeded the garden.	The garden *was weeded* by me.	The garden *was weeded*.

Scientific and documentary writing tends to use the passive voice more than other kinds of writing. This kind of writing often requires a high degree of objectivity and detachment, which can be achieved by erasing the agent and using the passive voice. Within these genres it is the process, rather than the person operating the process, that matters. Heavy use of the passive form results in a high degree of impersonality, which has its place when the writing needs to appear objective and professional, but when impersonality is taken too far it can lead to rather dehumanised writing. Many of the brochures and reports we read in the world of business are full of passive sentences working hard to erase any personalities behind the scenes. The 'house style' of any rule book is notoriously impersonal.

ACTIVITY 5:

Look at the following example of the use of the passive voice based on an extract from a university *Rules and Regulations* manual for students:

> Where a sponsor is a government agency, credit facilities will be given where confirmation of a fee payment liability has been received by completion of Form F257 or a letter from the organisation concerned. Such documentation must be presented at Registration.

Identify the passive constructions in the passage and assess why this particular writer has needed to use the passive voice. Find other examples of the institutional use of the passive voice and analyse why you think the passive voice has been used. Look at signs on doors, instruction books, rule books in your university or college.

ACTIVITY 6:

Write an autobiographical narrative of about 200 words telling the story of the first five years of your life. Use predominantly the passive voice. Why might the passive voice be awkward for writing autobiography? Is it easier to write in the passive voice about yourself as a child or as an adult?

We have given you a good deal of information about the verb element in clauses and the various forms that verb elements take. Before we go on to look at the subject element, check that you understand the following terms and expressions:

- transitive and intransitive verbs
- full verbs
- primary verbs
- auxiliaries
- modal verbs
- finite verbs
- non-finite verbs
- infinitive form
- verbs in the passive voice.

Inside the clause: the subject element

We have said that you cannot usually have a clause without a verb element (one word or several). We have called the verb the 'heart', or the 'nucleus', of the clause, around which other elements cluster. But there is one more element a clause must normally have. This is an expression of the person, thing or force which initiates the process, action or state that the verb expresses. This is what we call the agent or the *subject* of the clause – whatever sets the ball rolling. 'Agent' and 'subject' are function terms. In terms of form the agent can be expressed by one word or a phrase consisting of several words: a noun, pronoun or noun phrase. The formula of form and function would look like this:

Form: noun, pronoun or noun phrase
Function: subject or agent of the verb in the clause

So far we have said that the subject implies the idea of an 'agent': something or someone who makes something happen. But although many subject elements in clauses do express this idea of agency, we cannot say that all of them do. To explain this further we will divide subject elements into four different kinds as follows:

Types of subject element	Examples
Agent subjects: in which the subject is actively making something happen	*The Prime Minister* explained the new Children's Bill. *Many people* drive too fast. *Love* conquers all. *She* cooked us a big meal.
Identifier subjects: in which the subject is not an agent and the verb 'to be' is used to 'identify' something about the subject of the clause	*Kevin* is my brother. *The airport* was foggy. *Hilary* is a very good student.
Experiencer subjects: in which the subject is not making something happen but a comment is being made about the subject's experience	*I* liked the book. *She* could taste the garlic in the soup. *I* thought that you were not coming.
Nominal subjects: in which the words 'it' and 'there' are used in the subject positions, often with the verb 'to be', but don't have any substantial meaning and so are called 'nominal' subjects; they are used because clause grammar requires a word or phrase in the subject position	*There* is a car blocking the drive. *There* was such a loud noise coming from next door. Is *there* any soup? *It* is ten o'clock. *It* is time we went home.

In nearly all the examples we have listed above, the subject has been expressed by one word or one word accompanied by 'the'. However, just like the verb element, the subject element can also be made up of several words. Look at the following examples of subjects made up of several words – we have identified the main or central word in each one:

Subject element	Verb element
The *girl*	shouted.
The *girl* in the boat	shouted.
The blond *girl* in the striped pyjamas in the boat	shouted.

A long or short subject like this is characterised by having one *key* or *head word* and other kinds of words clustering around the head word, both before and after it. You can often tell, in practice, that the subject element has ended because the verb usually comes straight after it.

ACTIVITY 7:

- In an earlier activity you identified the verbs in a passage from Chinua Achebe's *Things Fall Apart*. Now identify the subjects of each of those verbs. You should find this easy as long as you do not expect the subject always to come first in a clause or sentence (contextual phrases often come first; they are adverbials as you will see later in the chapter). Most, but not all, of the subjects are agents.
- The following sentences all have a lengthy phrase as the subject of the verb. Find the verb, then the subject, then identify the key or head word in the phrase:

The large brown dog barked.
The sandwich shop across the road provided the sandwiches.
A sense of honour persisted in the family.
His passionate and evangelical preaching was popular with the congregation.
The tall willow tree swayed violently in the storm.
The noisy and threatening swarm came late that summer.
The committee's draconian judgements caused considerable controversy.

Note that in these examples the subject always comes to the left of the verb. In other words, the subject comes immediately before the verb. This is usually, but not always, the case in sentence construction.

Inside the clause: the adverbial

At the beginning of the chapter we defined the adverbial function as 'modifying the verb'. In other words, it adds extra detail about the circumstance within which the verb operates. It 'adds to' the verb (hence ad-verbial). Here is an example of a sentence with several adverbial elements:

At tea-time she arrived on the verandah, breathlessly.

Here is the sentence broken down to show the adverbial elements:

Adverbial	Subject	Verb	Adverbial	Adverbial
At tea-time	she	arrived	on the verandah	breathlessly.

The adverbials modify the verb because they specify:

- *when* she arrived ('at tea-time')
- *where* she arrived ('on the verandah')
- *how* she arrived ('breathlessly').

The sentence above contains a subject, a verb and three adverbials in the following order: adverbial element, subject element, verb element, adverbial element, adverbial element (ASVAA). You could rearrange it very easily to make it SVAAA:

Subject	Verb	Adverbial	Adverbial	Adverbial
She	arrived	on the verandah	at tea-time	breathlessly.

So the adverbials are very mobile in most clauses. However, if you try to change the positions of the subject and verb, you are more likely to construct an awkward or grammatically incorrect sentence like this:

Verb	Subject	Adverbial	Adverbial	Adverbial
Arrived	she	on the verandah	at tea-time	breathlessly.

The inversion of the subject and the verb in this sentence is simply ungrammatical because no native speaker would put the subject and verb in this order.

What can we say about adverbials generally?

- Although adverbials are not an essential part of a clause (like the subject and verb), they are extremely common.
- Adverbials can be used in just about any position in the clause – they are much more mobile than other elements of the clause.
- There can be more than one adverbial in a clause.
- An adverbial can be expressed by one word or several.

You have to be constantly on the look-out for adverbials, especially because they behave differently in number and position from all the other clause elements. You have probably already found that when you are looking for the subject in clauses you often have to leap-frog an opening group of words before you come to the subject. These clusters of words at the beginnings of sentences are often adverbials.

Adverbials tell us about, for example, the manner, space and time in which something occurred. Here are some simple examples in table form:

Manner	He wrote *rapidly*.	This tells us about the *way* in which he was writing.
Place	He worked *in the courtyard*.	This tells us about *where* he was working.
Time	*After dinner*, he *always* takes a stroll.	There are two adverbials here, telling us about *when* he takes a stroll and *how often*.

The formula of form and function looks like this:

Form: adverbs, adverbial phrases and prepositional phrases (see Chapters 3 and 4)
Function: to modify or add extra detail to the verb

We have referred to *prepositional phrases* in the table above as being adverbial in function. We will go into more detail in the next chapter about prepositions and prepositional phrases. For the moment we will simply tell you that a prepositional phrase begins with a preposition, a category or class of words which include 'in', 'across', 'under', 'besides'.

If you were analysing this sentence:

He walked *in the courtyard*.

in terms of phrase structure (which we will be explaining in Chapter 4), then 'in the courtyard' is a 'prepositional phrase' because it is a phrase which begins with a preposition ('in'). However, the phrase also acts as an adverbial of place because it is telling us where he walked. It is serving the *adverbial function* of the sentence. So if we say 'across the road' is a prepositional phrase we are describing and classifying the class of phrase it is. If we describe it as being adverbial we are describing the function it serves in the sentence. At this stage all you need to know is that this element of the clause is adverbial because it is adding circumstantial detail to the verb.

ACTIVITY 8:

Some writers and certain genres use a high number of adverbials; others use fewer or perhaps none at all. 'The Story' (from *Frog and Toad are Friends*) for example uses very few adverbials. We have taken a number of clauses and broken them down in order to identify the adverbials. Read our examples then complete the two unfinished tables below:

Examples of adverbials:

Adverbial (time)	Adverbial (place)	Subject	Verb
That night	in Max's room	a forest	grew ...

Adverbial (time)	Adverbial (place)	Adverbial (place)	Adverbial (place and distance)	Subject	Verb
Then	all around	from far away	across the river	he	heard ... (an echoing cry).

Unfinished tables for completion:

She	rushed off	through the woods	and under the moon	and in and out the dusky bluebells.

the thought of love would be ambered over with snow and winter; with log fires burning; with Russian women, gold swords, and the bark of stags (Woolf 1993: 69)

Adverbials in action

Here is a description of London at night during the Second World War from a short story called 'Mysterious Kor' by Elizabeth Bowen, first published in

1946. Bowen describes London through the eyes of two characters, as if it were some surreal city, lit and transformed by moonlight. She achieves this partly by describing the action of the people moving around the city, as if it were in slow motion or underwater. The information she gives us about how they move seems to retard the action and to give it a dreamlike quality.

> Outside the now gateless gates of the park, the road coming downhill from the north-west turned south and became a street, down whose perspective the traffic lights went through their unmeaning performance of changing colour. From the promontory of pavement outside the gates you saw at once up the road and down the street: from behind where you stood, between the gate-posts, appeared the lesser strangeness of grass and water and trees. At this point, at this moment, three French soldiers, directed to a hostel they could not find, stopped singing to listen derisively to the waterbirds wakened up by the moon. Next, two wardens coming off duty emerged from their post and crossed the road diagonally, each with an elbow cupped inside a slung-on tin hat. The wardens turned their faces, mauve in the moonlight, towards the Frenchmen with no expression at all. The two sets of steps died in opposite directions, and, the birds subsiding, nothing was seen or heard until, a little way down the street, a trickle of people came out of the underground, around the anti-panic brick wall.
>
> (Bowen 1987: 32–3)

In this passage and in other descriptive passages throughout the story, Bowen uses a huge number of adverbials expressed by single words or phrases to define further her description of actions, states and processes. Here is part of the passage again. For added clarity, we have identified all the finite and non-finite verbs by putting them into uppercase. Then we have put all the adverbials in the passage (which include single-word adverbs, adverbial phrases and prepositional phrases) into italic. You will see that Bowen uses a large number of adverbials in both finite and non-finite clauses. Even from a quick glance you can see what proportion of her sentences is made up with information that 'adds to' the verbs.

> *From the promontory of pavement outside the gates* you SAW *at once up the road* and *down the street: from behind where you stood, between the gate-posts,* APPEARED the lesser strangeness of grass and water and trees. *At this point, at this moment,* three French soldiers, DIRECTED to a hostel they COULD NOT FIND, STOPPED SINGING TO LISTEN *derisively* to the waterbirds WAKENED UP *by the moon. Next,* two wardens COMING off duty EMERGED *from their post* and CROSSED the road *diagonally,* each with an elbow cupped inside a slung-on tin hat. The wardens TURNED their faces, mauve in the moonlight, *towards the Frenchmen with no expression at all.*
>
> (Bowen 1987: 32–3)

ACTIVITY 9:

- Identify the subject of all the main verbs in the sentences above.
- Find examples of adverbials of manner, place or time.
- Find examples of non-finite clauses.
- Write out the passage in full sentences without using any adverbs or adverbial phrases. You may need to adjust the phrasing a little here and there.
- Now compare the new passage to the original. What effect does the omission of adverbs create?

As you can see from the above passage, adverbials can cluster around the verb in many different ways. Adverbials are the most mobile element in the clause and therefore the writer can play around with their position until he or she feels that they are in the right place.

ACTIVITY 10:

Experiment with the position of the adverbials in the following two sentences from Bowen's story by rearranging them. See how many different versions of the sentences you can come up with. How have the sentences changed as a result of your rearrangement in terms of emphasis or even meaning?

> *Next*, two wardens COMING off duty EMERGED *from their post* and CROSSED the road *diagonally*, each with an elbow cupped inside a slung-on tin hat. The wardens TURNED their faces, mauve in the moonlight, *towards the Frenchmen with no expression at all*.

The split infinitive

Although we have said the adverbial can go almost anywhere in the sentence, many people strongly object to the use of an adverbial between 'to' and the infinite form of the verb. This is called the *split infinitive* construction. The most famous example comes from what we might call the 'mission statement' of the Starship Enterprise in the television programme *Star Trek*:

> . . . *to boldly go* where no man has gone before

(In *Star Trek: The Next Generation* of course this was changed to 'To boldly go where no one has gone before'.) 'To go' is the infinitive form of the verb 'go' and the adverb 'boldly' has been inserted between the two parts of the verb. Some people argue that 'the unity of the infinitive' should not be broken; others argue, more subjectively, that such split infinitives just sound 'ugly'. Some time ago Radio Four initiated a debate about the use of the split infinitive and many people agreed that, as the rule is now more often broken than it is observed, it is a redundant rule. Some people still continue to have strong feelings about it, however. This book, as we have said, is not a prescriptive grammar book, but an explorative one. So all we will say here is that the construction is frequently used in speech and sometimes it is difficult to avoid splitting the infinitive in writing.

Inside the clause: the direct object

By the direct object of the clause we refer to the person or thing directly affected by the action expressed by the verb. This often comes straight after the verb and, like the subject element, takes the form of a noun, pronoun or noun phrase. Just as for the subject element, when we talk of the object we are talking about the function of the word or group of words. When we say it is made up of a noun or noun phrase we are referring to the form of the word or group of words:

Form: noun, pronoun, or noun phrase (see Chapters 3 and 4)
Function: direct object of the verb

Here is a series of examples of direct objects in short sentences (they are all SVO in structure):

Subject	Verb	Direct object
Kezia	peeled	the orange.
I	saw	the sea.
The gleaners	gathered	the corn.
Max	wore	his wolf suit.
He	made	mischief.
They	roared	their terrible roars.
He	smelled	good things to eat.

Adverbial or direct object?

It is sometimes difficult to distinguish between an adverbial and a direct object in a clause. It is those small linking words like 'to', 'in', and 'after' (prepositions) which create the difficulty. The question you have to answer is: does the 'to' or 'in' attach to the verb in meaning or the group of words after the verb? For example, in the following examples the particle after the verb is part of the meaning of the verb:

Subject	Verb	Direct object
He	is bringing up	two small children.
I've	handed in	my resignation.
She	put up with	a lot of teasing.
Her company	paid for	her driving lessons.

In the following examples the small linking words belong not to the verb but to the adverbial that comes after it.

Subject	Verb	Adverbial
He	walked	in the courtyard. (adverbial of place)
I	stayed	for a week. (adverbial of time)
I	ate	with my fork. (adverbial of manner)

ACTIVITY 11:

Find the subject element, verb element and direct object and adverbials (where appropriate) in the following sentences or clauses from Bessie Head's short story 'Looking for a Rain God' from *A Collector of Treasures* (1977).

Only the charlatans, incanters, and witch-doctors made a pile of money during this time.
They experienced all kinds of things once they left the village.
They did not even hear the funny chatter.
The goats had started producing milk . . .
People in the village soon noted the absence of the two little girls.
The police asked to see the graves.

(Head 1977: 57)

Inside the clause: the indirect object

For the practical purposes of writing and analysing texts, the four clause elements (subject, verb, adverbial and direct object) are the most important ones to be aware of that we have explained so far. We shall deal with the remaining three more briefly. As we explained earlier, there are two kinds of object in a sentence: a *direct object* and an *indirect object*. In a sentence like:

> The Ministry of Defence sent a report to the Prime Minister.

what was actually sent was 'the report' not 'the Prime Minister', but it was sent *to* the Prime Minister; so 'report' is the direct object of the verb 'sent' and Prime Minister is the indirect object. This is what it looks like mapped out alongside some other examples:

Subject	Verb	Direct object	Indirect object
The Ministry of Defence	sent	a report	to the Prime Minister.
I	gave	a ring	to my friend.
Toad	gave	a cup of tea	to Frog.
I	should give	a drink	to the baby.

Inside the clause: the subject complement

The final two optional elements of any clause are called *complements: subject complements*, which add meaning, detail and definition to the subject; and *object complements*, which add meaning, detail or definition to the object. (Complement means 'completes the meaning of'.) For example:

> You look ill.

The word 'ill' is a complement, but is it an object complement or a subject complement? What other part of the clause does the word 'ill' tell you more about? It tells us more about the word 'you', which is the subject of the verb 'look'.

The following sentence is different:

> She made me angry.

In this sentence 'angry' is the complement but it tells us more about the direct object of the verb ('me') rather than more about the subject ('She'). In this case 'angry' is therefore an object complement.

In the following sentence, 'He' (the subject) is followed by 'is' (the verb), and then a noun phrase which adds to the meaning of 'He': 'he is a doctor'.

Subject	Verb	Subject complement
He	is	a doctor.

Compare this with the following sentence:

Subject	Verb	Direct object
Kezia	peeled	the orange.

Now 'the orange' here is the direct object, not complement, because 'the orange' does not add to or complete the meaning of 'Kezia'. Kezia is not, in any sense, an orange. The orange is the 'direct object' of the verb 'peeled'.

Subject complements are found with a small group of verbs which precisely link a subject and its complement. These verbs are called *linking* or *copular verbs*.

Linking verb	Example
To be	I *am* cold. I *am* a doctor.
To seem	He *seemed* angry.
To feel	I *feel* foolish.
To appear	They *appeared* frustrated.
To grow	He *grew* pale.
To remain	She *remained* silent.
To turn	Simon *turned* pale.
To become	They *became* angry.
To sound	The party *sounded* great.
To taste	The chicken *tasted* burnt.
To turn	The crowd *turned* nasty.
To look	She *looked* sour-faced.
To get	I *get* cross.
To go	He *went* quiet.
To prove	The meeting *proved* successful. The meeting *proved* a disaster.

Complements can be both adjectives and nouns. For example:

Subject	Verb	Subject complement (adjective)
She	is	happy.

Subject	Verb	Subject complement (noun)
He	is	a singer.

Inside the clause: the object complement

If an adverb adds to the verb, and a subject complement adds to the subject, then it follows that an object complement adds to the object. Object complements do indeed come after the object in a clause and add to the meaning of the object word or phrase. For example:

Subject	Verb	Object	Object complement
They	found	the house	too expensive.
She	made	me	angry.

In these examples, the complement words (or phrases) are 'too expensive' and 'angry'. You can see which part of the clause each complements or 'adds to'. It is not 'They' who are expensive, it is 'the house', the object of the clause. Equally, it is not 'she' who is angry, but 'me' the object. Here are two more examples of object complements:

Subject	Verb	Object	Object complement
The Prime Minister's secretary	has left	all his letters	unopened.
The committee	has elected	you	chairperson.

Here are two examples which show the difference between subject complements and object complements:

Subject	Verb	Subject complement
Jim	is becoming	quite confident.

Subject	Verb	Object	Object complement
Pat	considers	Jim	quite confident.

ACTIVITY 12:

Each of the following sentences has either a subject complement or an object complement. Identify them. Remember: if you identify the subject and object of the sentence first, and decide if the verb is a linking verb, then it will be easier to tell whether the complement adds to the subject, or adds to the object.

That was a very interesting play.
She found the summer winds too hot and dry.
Sarah was a doctor.
The responsibility is too much.
I found the play boring.
You are looking quite green.
I am a frog.

More dependent clauses

Now that we have explored in some detail all the seven different clause elements, we are going to turn, as promised, to identifying different kinds of dependent clause. Being able to recognise and identify these is an important part of language work and being aware of how and where they can be used will enhance your own command of written language. We pointed out in Chapter 1 that, although there could only be one kind of independent clause (by definition), there are several kinds of dependent clause, and we said we would describe some of these at the end of this chapter. We shall assume that you have studied this section before you move on to Chapter 3.

Adverbial clauses

In Chapter 1, the dependent clauses we presented were all ones introduced by subordinating conjunctions (such as 'after', 'until', 'so', 'as', 'because'). We can now tell you that such subordinate clauses are *adverbial in function*. Let us examine a dependent clause introduced by a subordinating conjunction:

> That night out in the yard the dog howled until Hannah eventually let him into the house.

Main (independent) clause	Subordinate (dependent) clause with an adverbial function
That night out in the yard the dog howled	until Hannah eventually let him into the house.

The verb in the main clause is 'howled' and the dependent clause adds the idea of a point in time being reached in the dog's howling; therefore the 'until'-clause modifies the verb and so is an adverbial clause in function. There are over forty of these subordinating conjunctions which make the clauses they introduce adverbial clauses. David Crystal in his *Rediscover Grammar* (1996) gives a useful table of subordinating conjunctions and the adverbial meanings they express with simple examples. Here, again, is an adaptation of his table:

Subordinating conjunctions	Examples	Meanings they express
After, as, before, since, till, until, when, while	I rang while you were out.	Time
Where, wherever	I'll see where he is.	Place
If, unless, in case, as long as, supposing	I'll go if you come with me.	Condition
Whereas, whilst, while	I can dance, whereas you can't.	Contrast
Except, but that, save that, excepting that	I'd go, except that I don't have the time.	Exception
Because, since, for	I can't go, because it's expensive.	Reason
To, in order to, so as to	I left early, in order to pick up my children.	Purpose
So, so that	She was hungry, so she ordered a pizza.	Result
As, like	Do as I say.	Similarity
As if, as though, like	It looks as if he's in.	Comparison
The . . . the	The more I do, the less I like it.	Proportion
Rather than, sooner than	I'd walk rather than go on a horse.	Preference

(From Crystal 1996: 205)

Nominal clauses

We have already said that subject and direct object elements can be expressed by one word or several. For example:

Subject element	Verb element	Direct object element
That meal	disagreed with	me.
His words	hurt	me.
The book's future	depends upon	the reviewers of the journals.
I	don't know	his future plans.

It is possible to replace these subject and object elements with one complete clause (a nominal clause) containing at least a subject and finite verb. We shall show you how by converting the sentences above and identifying the nominal clauses in italic. Notice the use of 'what', 'that' and 'how' to introduce these replacement clauses. Notice too how a verb remains the nucleus of the new dependent clause and the main clause structure. Compare the following, then, with their originals above:

Subject element	Verb element	Direct object
What I ate	disagreed with	me.
What he said	hurt	me.
How the book will sell	depends upon	*how the reviewers react.*
I	don't know	*what he intends to do.*

Clauses which replace subject and object elements like this are, of course, subordinate clauses: they cannot stand on their own and make a complete meaning. Such clauses are often called *nominal* clauses because they replace nouns or noun phrases and 'nominal' means 'noun-like'.

Relative clauses

A relative clause is a dependent clause which modifies the noun or noun phrase that precedes it. In the following sentence the relative clause is identified in italic:

The watch *that I bought* has broken.

The phrase 'that I bought' gives extra information about the watch: it is that specific watch 'that I bought'. This kind of dependent clause is called a *relative clause* because it relates to, in this case, the subject of the main verb. In this example it has been inserted as an additional piece of information about the subject ('the watch') between the subject and the verb ('has broken'). Even so it is a full clause, with a noun, or pronoun, and a verb, but it is a subordinate clause. In other words it is dependent. If we tried to see whether it would stand alone as a sentence like this:

> that I bought

we can see that it can't be independent because it is incomplete. Relative clauses like this are extremely common in all kinds of writing (and in the spoken language too).

Relative clauses are introduced by a small group of words, called *relative pronouns* – relative because they 'relate to' the noun phrase. These are 'who', 'whom' (formal), 'whose', 'which', 'that', and 'zero' (see below for an explanation of this one). Here are some simple examples:

> The man *who spoke yesterday* will speak again tomorrow.
> Can I see the official *to whom I spoke*?
> I have read the books *that are on the shelf.*
> That film *I told you about* isn't on any more.

Note that in the final example the relative pronoun, which normally signals a relative clause, has been left out even though the highlighted clause is certainly a relative clause (this is what 'zero' refers to). Native speakers of English instinctively know when the relative pronoun can be left out.

Non-finite clauses

We have already discussed non-finite clauses in this chapter, in our exploration of verb functions and forms. Here are some examples:

> *Hastening through the crowd,* Mr Samuels saw his mother in the distance.
> *Tripping on his shoe laces,* Mr Samuels lurched towards Mrs Jones.
> *Recovered from his fall,* Mr Samuels apologised to Mrs Jones.

Non-finite dependent clauses are common in many kinds of writing so it is important that you are aware of them. We suggest you return to the earlier part of the chapter for a brief revision and consolidation.

Summary

In this chapter we have

- examined the seven key elements of the clause:
  - verb
  - subject
  - adverbial
  - direct object
  - indirect object
  - subject complement
  - object complement
- explored the way in which these elements are used to create certain effects in writing
- described several types of dependent clause and their function:
  - adverbial clauses
  - nominal clauses
  - relative clauses
  - non-finite clauses

References

Achebe, Chinua (1986) *Things Fall Apart* [1958]. African Writers Series. Oxford: Heinemann.

Bowen, Elizabeth (1987) 'Mysterious Kor' [1946] in Malcolm Bradbury (ed.), *The Penguin Book of Short Stories*. Harmondsworth: Penguin.

Crystal, David (1996) *Rediscover Grammar*. Harlow: Longman.

Head, Bessie (1977) 'Looking for a Rain God' in *The Collector of Treasures*. London: Heinemann.

O'Brien, Tim (1990) 'The Things they Carried' in *The Things they Carried*. Harmondsworth: Penguin.

Woolf, Virginia (1993) *Orlando* [1928] Harmondsworth: Penguin.

Wordsworth, William (1993) 'The Tables Turned' in M.H. Abrams (ed.), *Norton Anthology of English Literature*, Vol. 2. London: W.W. Norton & Co.

Word grammar

Rebecca Stott and Peter Chapman

In the last two chapters we have introduced you to the basic grammatical constructions of sentences; in Chapter 1 we showed you how clauses are joined together in various ways within sentences and in Chapter 2 we showed how each element inside the clause achieves one of seven possible key functions. Now we are going to focus on words and word classes.

Word functions

Words carry meanings, but in order to fit successfully together in sentences, words have to be able to do different jobs – perform different functions. There is a kind of 'division of labour' between words. There are, at this foundational level of language, about eight different functions that we need words to perform for us (it is possible to subdivide one or two of these classes, producing a number of classes greater than eight, but this is not necessary for our purposes). These functions are spread across the *word classes* of English, and what we are now going to discuss is word classification.

The labels for word classification will probably not be entirely new to you and we have mentioned some of them already in this book: 'conjunction', 'noun', 'verb' and 'adverb' in particular. Our aim in this chapter is twofold: to show you how words are grouped into word classes and to show you how such knowledge might be useful to you both as a reader of literature and as a writer.

Word classes and the work they do: an overview

The language network	
Noun	Used for naming persons or things or places or abstractions (e.g. Vikram, woman, house, car, Edinburgh, love, fear)
Adjective	Used to modify a noun by adding to its meaning (e.g. hungry, kind, sad, blue, hairy, adventurous)
Pronoun	Used instead of a noun or noun phrase (e.g. he, it, they, mine, who)
Verb	Used to express an action, state or process (e.g. play, go, be, have, do, weep, may, can, satisfy, fight)
Adverb	Used to modify or add to the verb (e.g. quickly, laboriously, today, often)
Preposition	Used to express a relationship between nouns or other word classes, often of space or time (e.g. on, to, in, under, above, at, beyond)
Conjunction	Used either to co-ordinate words, phrases and clauses (co-ordinating conjunctions) or to introduce subordinate clauses (subordinating conjunctions) (e.g. and, but, or, if, before, because, except)
Determiner	Used to indicate the scope of a noun (e.g. a, the, that, some, any)

All words in every sentence can be classified according to this list of eight classes. The eight classes can be further divided into two groups which we call *open* and *closed word classes*.

Open classes	Closed classes
Nouns	Pronouns
Adjectives	Conjunctions
Verbs*	Prepositions
Adverbs	Determiners

* Note: Strictly speaking, verbs fall into both the open and the closed categories, as we have already implied in the last chapter. Full verbs are open class; primary and modal verbs are closed class.

Broadly speaking, closed word classes remain fixed and unchanging, whereas open word classes are constantly changing and evolving. We have to have *open* word classes (nouns, adjectives, verbs and adverbs) to allow new ideas to be expressed, and to allow no-longer-useful ideas to fade away. For example, nouns and names for things change from generation to generation. The writers of dictionaries have to decide each time they update a dictionary which new words have entered the language and are likely to stay there. Some words are forgotten because new words replace them. 'Wireless', for instance, is now almost obsolete because it has been replaced by the word 'radio'. The word 'beau' once meant 'boyfriend' but would not be used by today's teenagers, nor would the word 'courting' – except perhaps ironically. We need words which reflect the world around us and currently compilers of dictionaries are busy adding new words and phrases such as 'disk drive', 'gender-bending' and 'sourcing'. New words introduce new concepts: the word 'environment', for instance, now such an important word, was not coined until the early nineteenth century. Words change as society and ideas change.

We also need words to act as a kind of glue or cement to hold these express-ive words together in logical and systematic ways and this is what the *closed* word classes do. The closed word classes like pronouns ('he', 'she', 'they'), conjunctions ('and', 'but', 'or', 'if', 'because'), prepositions ('above', 'below', 'to', 'up', 'under') and determiners ('a', 'the') do not change, broadly speak-ing, although we could argue that in the much longer term some of these have altered in the past and will do in the future. We only have to glance back a few hundred years to see that pronouns were once rather different ('thee', 'thou') and to notice that we have now adopted the form of 's/he' in much writing to avoid being sexist in our use of language. Generally though, the words that change and evolve are the open word classes and closed word classes mostly stay the same.

We say that English has eight word classes because words do eight dif-ferent things for us. We shall describe these things in a moment, but first we must raise a crucial question. Does the fact that there are eight word classes mean that every word in our language fits into just one of these classes? Very significantly, the answer is no. Many words are adaptable and can move around from class to class. Take, for example, the word 'round'. Even before we have explained the functions of the word classes, you can quickly see that 'round' can 'move around' in clauses and sentences. It can be adapted to different classes: it can be a verb, a noun, an adjective, an adverb and a preposition, depending upon its place in the clause. For example:

Look through the *round* window. (adjective)
It's your *round*, Gerry. Mine's a pint! (noun)
The racing car swerved as it *rounded* the first bend. (verb)
Round the corner came the carnival procession. (preposition)
Walking *round* to the post office, I met Robin. (adverb)

To give you another example: the colourless little word 'that' is amazingly ver-satile. Look it up in a good dictionary and look up the code letters for word classes at the front of the dictionary to see how many word classes 'that' can belong to. Dictionaries are full of grammatical information if used skilfully.

Many words, then, are like good actors who can play a number of dif-ferent roles. Now that we have identified the eight different word classes (or roles), we will describe the work that they do in much more detail. We will begin with the four open word classes: noun, adjective, verb and adverb. For examples we will present passages of published prose and also attempt to breathe new life into the old favourite of many primary schools a few generations ago: 'the cat sat on the mat'.

Open word classes: the noun

Words in this class are used for naming some person, place, thing or abstraction. We need to be able to refer to objects and structures in the world and concepts inside our heads (and, as we have said, the ways all these change and shift). We need to be able to say whether these are countable (like bottles of wine) or uncountable (like flour, or sunshine, or love). We need words to name people and places and institutions. When words are doing this kind of work they are called *nouns*. They can be concrete, abstract, singular or plural, or they can be the names of people or places.

> The *cat* sits on the *mat*.
> This *cat* eats *cheese*.
> This *cat* plays *chess*.
> This *cat* is full of *wisdom*.
> This *cat* lives in the *House of Commons* in *London*.

Pronouns are words used to stand in for a noun or for a noun phrase. We deal with these more fully later in the chapter but it is useful to mention them here to show their relationship with nouns. Here are some examples:

> *He* walked uneasily past *her*.
> *I*'d like the red *one* please.
> Look at *that*. *He* must be mad!

Personal Pronouns are the words we use to stand in for nouns when they are being used either as subjects ('I', 'he', 'they', 'we') or objects ('me', 'us', 'them').

Nouns in action

Here is a passage from a nineteenth-century novel by Charles Kingsley called *Alton Locke: Tailor and Poet* (1850). Like many nineteenth-century novelists, Kingsley used the novel to draw attention to poverty and the social conditions of the poor. In this passage he describes a London slum. Inevitably, Kingsley uses a large number of nouns, which we have identified in italic:

> It was a foul, chilly, foggy Saturday *night*. From the *butchers'* and *greengrocers' shops* the *gaslights* flared and flickered, wild and ghastly, over haggard *groups* of slipshod dirty *women*, bargaining for stale *meat* and frost-bitten *vegetables*, wrangling about short *weight* and bad *quality*. Fish *stalls* and fruit *stalls* lined the *edge* of the greasy *pavement*, sending up *odours* as foul as the *language* of *sellers* and *buyers*. *Blood* and sewer *water* crawled from under *doors* and out of *spouts*, and reeked down the *gutters* among *offal*, animal and vegetable, in every *stage* of *putrefaction*. Foul *vapours* rose from cow *sheds* and *slaughterhouses*, and the *doorways* of undrained *alleys*, where the *inhabitants* carried the *filth* out on their *shoes* from the *backyard* into the *court*, and from the *court* up into the main *street*; while above, hanging like *cliffs* over the *streets* – those narrow, brawling *torrents* of *filth*, and *poverty* and *sin* – the *houses* with their teeming *load* of *life* were piled up into the dingy, choking *night*. A ghastly, deafening, sickening *sight* it was. Go, scented *Belgravian*! And see what *London* is!
>
> (Kingsley 1892: 66)

There are a high number of concrete nouns in this passage as we would expect. Kingsley is describing a slum and as he wants his largely middle-class readers to see what he sees, he gives lots of detail about physical things such as the place itself (its shops, alleys, courtyards, streets, houses, backyards, sheds and slaughterhouses) and the objects and people within the place (the gaslights, meat, vegetables, stalls, women, sellers and buyers, offal, doors, spouts, gutters, blood and sewer water and so on). All these things are tangible objects and so we call the nouns that refer to such things *concrete nouns* because they refer to concrete (physical) things. He uses other nouns such as 'vapours' and 'odours' to make us imagine how the slum smells. But Kingsley wants us to see beyond the physical world he describes to terrible abstract things too which we can't actually see or touch and he uses *abstract nouns* such as 'putrefaction' (rotting), 'poverty' and 'sin' to describe these.

When we identify the nouns in a passage of descriptive writing like this we can see much more clearly *how* Kingsley has painted his picture and what objects in particular he has picked out for us to see. By mixing objects like meat and vegetables, for instance, with blood and sewer water and putrefaction, he can show very starkly how unsanitary these conditions are – so crowded and choking that food is contaminated by its proximity to excrement and blood. Filth is carried into every corner. No one could stay clean, healthy or perhaps even hopeful in such conditions.

However, Kingsley does not achieve all of his effects from nouns alone. In order to describe the scene in detail he needs to be more specific about the objects he depicts and for this he needs the support of adjectives.

Open word classes: the adjective

Words in this class are used to express some feature or quality of a noun. Adjectives modify nouns. When writers need to add extra detail to nouns they will use adjectives, sometimes one, sometimes several, depending on the final effect required: for example, '*dusty* bottles of wine'; '*self-raising* flour'; '*glorious, warming* sunshine'; '*heavenly* love'. The words in italic are acting here as adjectives.

Adjectives are most commonly used in two positions in a clause: one position is in front of a noun and the second position is after verbs like 'to seem' or 'to become'. These verbs are called 'linking verbs' because they bring together a noun or pronoun and an adjective as in 'the road was narrow', 'he seems tired', 'petrol is becoming expensive'. Many adjectives can be made into adverbs simply by adding '–ly': for example, sad = sadly, cold = coldly.

Most adjectives have *comparative* and *superlative* forms:

good   better   best
large   larger   largest
famous   more famous   most famous

The *black* cat sits quietly on the *big* mat.
The *black* cat was *thin*.
The *black* cat was *hungry*.
The *black* cat was the *hungriest* cat in town.

Adjectives in action

Joseph Conrad, the Anglo-Polish novelist and author of *Heart of Darkness* (1899), is famous for using large, some say excessive, numbers of adjectives. The literary critic F.R. Leavis complained about Conrad's 'adjectival insistence', arguing that he used three or four adjectives where one would do. Here's just one example (with the adjectives italicised) from *Heart of Darkness*:

> We looked at the *venerable* stream not in the *vivid* flush of a *short* day that comes and departs for ever, but in the *august* light of *abiding* memories.

(Conrad 1981: 6)

'Adjectival insistence' has become one of the defining features of Conrad's prose style, but it is also a defining feature of much nineteenth-century writing. Virginia Woolf complained in her novel *Orlando* (1928) that Victorian writing was too verbose and that it was as if the sentences had become swollen by the damp which ruined so much furniture in the nineteenth century. Sometimes, however, adjectives are used to spectacular effect in nineteenth-century writing, such as in the writing of John Ruskin.

In the following passage, the nineteenth-century artist, writer, critic, poet and social commentator John Ruskin takes us on an imaginary journey northwards, flying like a bird from southern to northern Europe. His aim in the essay called 'The Savageness of Gothic Architecture' is to show that the art and architecture produced in southern Europe is different from that of northern Europe in part because of the differences in climate and landscape. Adjectives are therefore very important to Ruskin in helping to distinguish between the landscape of southern and northern Europe. This is how he describes Europe from his imaginary bird's-eye view. We have identified the adjectives in italic:

> Let us, for a moment . . . imagine the Mediterranean lying beneath us like an *irregular* lake, and all its *ancient* promontories sleeping in the sun: here and there an *angry* spot of thunder, a *grey* stain of storm, moving upon the *burning* field; and here and there a *fixed* wreath of *white volcano* smoke, surrounded by its circle of ashes; but for the most part a *great* peacefulness of light, Syria and Greece, Italy and Spain, laid like pieces of a *golden* pavement into the sea-blue,[1] chased[2] as we stoop nearer to them, with *bossy beaten* work of *mountain*[3] chains, and glowing softly with *terraced* gardens, and flowers *heavy* with frankincense, mixed among masses of laurel, and orange, and *plumy* palm, that abate with their *grey-green* shadows the burning of the *marble* rocks, and of the ledges of porphyry sloping under *lucent* sand. Then let us pass further towards the north, until we see the *orient* colours change gradually into a *vast* belt of *rainy* green, where the pastures of Switzerland, and *poplar* valleys of France, and *dark* forests of the Danube and Carpathian stretch from the mouths of the Loire to those of the Volga, seen through the clefts in *grey* swirls of *rain* cloud and *flaky* veils of the mist of the brooks, spreading low amongst the *pasture* lands: and then, further north still, to see the earth heave into *mighty* masses of *leaden* rock and *heathy* moor, bordering with a *broad* waste of *gloomy* purple that belt of field and wood, and splintering into *irregular* and *grisly* islands amidst the *northern* seas, beaten by storm, and chilled by *ice*

---

[1] 'Sea-blue' is usually used as an adjective: 'the sea-blue fence' for instance. Ruskin is using sea-blue as a noun here, however, as if the colour were something tangible into which pieces of a golden pavement are laid. It is a compound noun made from combining 'blue' (adjective) and 'sea' (noun), joined by a hyphen.

[2] A technical term meaning embossed.

[3] Here the word 'mountain', which is usually a noun, is being used as an adjective adding to 'chains'.

drift, and tormented by *furious* pulses of *contending* tide, until the roots of the *last* forests fail from among the *hill* ravines, and the hunger of the *north* wind bites their peaks into barrenness; and, at last, the wall of ice, *durable* like iron, sets, deathlike,[4] its *white* teeth against us out of the *polar* twilight.

(Ruskin 1995: 191)

Ruskin's use of prose is poetic: he is inventive with language and writes with an ear for rhythms and patterns of sound. Sometimes his adjectives seem to be chosen in order to create poetic effects, such as alliteration in phrases like 'bossy beaten work', 'plumy palm' and 'mighty masses', but there are other beautiful combinations of sound too, such as 'lucent sand' and 'grey stain of storm'. Ruskin is inventive with words and will turn a noun such as 'heath' into an adjective in order to achieve particular effects such as 'heathy moor'. Other unusual adjective and noun combinations are 'rainy green' and 'gloomy purple' and these reveal a painter's eye at work for he is very precise in the kinds of colours that he wants us to see. He is also interested in texture and shape when he tells us that the veils of the mist are 'flaky' (presumably this is the effect he perceives as an artist) and the palms are 'plumy' (i.e. like plumes).

These are all instances of Ruskin's creative use of adjectives but do they achieve the desired effect? Ruskin wants to persuade us that there is a connection between the landscapes of Europe and the kinds of art produced in its regions. If we divide up the main adjectives into two groups – those used to describe the south and those used to describe the north – we can see the differences that Ruskin wants us to see very starkly. We have not included the first adjectives of the passage such as 'angry' and 'grey' because Ruskin says they only occur 'here and there' in southern Europe:

Southern Europe	Northern Europe
ancient, burning, white, golden, bossy (meaning embossed), beaten, heavy, plumy, grey-green, lucent (full of light), marble	vast, rainy, dark, grey, rain, flaky, mighty, leaden, heathy, broad, gloomy, irregular, grisly, ice, furious, contending, durable, white, polar

Later in the essay Ruskin says it is not surprising that there is a certain 'wildness of thought and roughness of work' in the art of Northern Europe,

---

[4] 'Deathlike' is most often used as an adjective, e.g. 'deathlike silence', but here it functions as an adverb because it modifies the verb 'sets'.

'a magnificence of sturdy power', because these artists did not live in a naturally hospitable environment of abundant food and gentle sunshine, but had to 'break the rock for bread, and cleave the forest for fire'. But the adjectives he has collected together in his piece of what we might call word-painting, or prose-poetry, have already established the essential characteristics of southern and northern art.

In contrast to the adjectival richness of Ruskin's prose, many early twentieth-century writers produced a distinctively economical and spare prose. Ernest Hemingway, the American novelist, made it a working rule to go through what he had written each day and cross out all (or most) of the adjectives. Compare this example from his 1927 short story 'In Another Country' with the sentence from Conrad given above:

It was a *cold* fall and the wind came down from the mountains.

(Hemingway 1992: 89)

Hemingway was writing in the aftermath of the First World War and he felt he had to start all over again, to learn to write simply and truly as if for the first time. Hemingway said of his life in Paris in the 1920s: 'I was trying to learn to write, commencing with the simplest things . . . [to] put down what I see and what I feel in the best and simplest way I can tell it'. He broke with the dominant prose styles of much nineteenth-century writing, which he regarded as florid and overwritten, sentimental and loaded with far too many subordinate sentences. Hemingway was not the only early twentieth-century writer to use a simpler style. Gertrude Stein, another experimental American writer living in Paris at the same time, always believed that Hemingway had copied her style and made a fortune from it. But Hemingway was the first to enjoy critical success with this particular kind of sparse prose style, and he radically changed the public's taste in fiction. Many writers have mimicked and parodied his style since.

ACTIVITY 1:

Take the sentence 'The cat sat on the mat' and add unusual adjectives, suggestive and imaginative enough to work as an unconventional opening sentence to a children's story. Try writing a series of between five and ten sentences of this kind. You might want to add a few sentences to each saying what you imagine the full story might be about. Here's an example:

The *prosperous* and *corpulent* cat sat on his *jewelled* mat.

ACTIVITY 2:

Identify all the adjectives in the passage from *Alton Locke* (we've done the first three sentences). Are there more adjectives than nouns in the passage, or fewer? Write a list of all the adjectives. Comment on Kingsley's choice of adjectives and explain what his choice of adjectives has contributed to the effect of the passage as a whole. Now write out the passage without any adjectives and comment on the difference between the original and the revised versions.

It was a *foul, chilly, foggy Saturday** night. From the butchers' and greengrocers' shops the gaslights flared and flickered, *wild* and *ghastly*, over *haggard* groups of *slipshod dirty* women, bargaining for *stale* meat and *frost-bitten* vegetables, wrangling about *short* weight and *bad* quality. *Fish** stalls and *fruit** stalls lined the edge of the *greasy* pavement, sending up odours as *foul* as the language of sellers and buyers. Blood and sewer water crawled from under doors and out of spouts, and reeked down the gutters among offal, animal and vegetable, in every stage of putrefaction. Foul vapours rose from cow sheds and slaughterhouses, and the doorways of undrained alleys, where the inhabitants carried the filth out on their shoes from the backyard into the court, and from the court up into the main street; while above, hanging like cliffs over the streets – those narrow, brawling torrents of filth, and poverty and sin – the houses with their teeming load of life were piled up into the dingy, choking night. A ghastly, deafening, sickening sight it was. Go, scented Belgravian! And see what London is!

(Kingsley 1892: 66)

ACTIVITY 3:

Think about how you would set about writing in the style of Ruskin or Kingsley either because you admire their styles or because you want to parody them. Write a piece of about 150–200 words on a car or train journey through a region you know or can imagine. Be conscious of noun and adjective choices in particular. Add a short commentary saying what you were trying to do.

---

* These words could be classified as either adjectives or nouns. The same is true of '*sewer* water' and '*cow* sheds'. In the phrases 'butchers' shops' and 'grocers' shops' the words butchers' and grocers' are in the possessive so they are working more strictly as nouns rather than adjectives.

Open word classes: the verb

Words in this class are used to refer to actions, processes or states. We have already looked at verbs in some detail in the last chapter but we'll repeat some of the points here by way of consolidation. Writing a letter is an action (it needs energy and effort), so is playing a guitar; but being tired and having a headache are not actions but states; both actions and states are expressed by verbs. In order to give us more information about when these actions or states took place in time, verbs take tenses: 'he went', 'he goes', 'he will go'. Strictly speaking, there is no future tense form in English as there is a present tense form 'goes/go' and past tense 'went'. English expresses future meaning by:

- using present tense: 'I am going next week'
- using 'going to': 'I am going to buy that book'
- using will/shall + base: 'I will go tomorrow'.

Verbs are often one word but they are equally often more than one word. Here is an extreme example to make the point: 'I *should have been enjoying* myself today'. In this example, the main verb is 'enjoying' and the other three underlined words are auxiliary or 'helping' verbs. We discussed this in the last chapter, of course.

> The cat *sits* on the mat.
> The cat *has been meditating* on the mat.
> The cat *will fly* on the mat.
> The cat *reads* Spinoza on the mat.

Verbs in action

By way of contrast to the pieces of fictional descriptive writing we have looked at in the book so far, here is a rather different piece of descriptive writing from *The Collins Bird Guide* which has a surprisingly poetic quality to it and which is very economical in its description of the movements of the birds described. We have identified the verbs in italic:

> Purple Gallinule: Rather shy, the Purple Gallinule *spends* much time inside reedbeds or, in Africa, in papyrus swamps, but also *feeds* along the fringes, *walking* in and out of the vegetation at any time of day. In the evening it often *clambers up** stems of reeds or papyrus and *sits up** in the open, surveying the landscape.

> (Keith and Gooders 1980: 446)

---

* Both these verbs have prepositions attached to them: 'clamber up' and 'sit up'.

Dunlin: The active little waders *feed* busily, *probing* this way and that as they *wade* across shallow pools or *follow* the tide line. They sometimes *gather* in immense numbers at favoured feeding grounds and *will form* dense packs in flight. They alternately *show* white, then dark, as they *twist* and *turn* in unison in the air.

(Keith and Gooders 1980: 476)

The task of the writers is to sum up in two or three sentences the characteristic behaviour of the particular bird and to achieve this they must include as many verbs in each sentence as possible. They could have made rather a dull list of these activities by using co-ordinate sentences with clauses joined by 'and' such as:

Dunlin: The active little waders *feed* busily and *probe* this way and that and *wade* across shallow pools and *follow* the tide line. They sometimes *gather* in immense numbers at favoured feeding grounds and *form* dense packs in flight. They alternately *show* white, then dark, and they *twist* and *turn* in unison in the air.

But the writer here is more skilful and can bring all these activities together by using verbs in a variety of different ways within main and subordinate clauses. The first verb is active and finite (they 'feed'); the second verb is in a non-finite form ('probing this way and that') and describes how they feed; the third and fourth verbs ('as they *wade* . . . or *follow*) are in finite form but within a subordinate clause ('*as* they wade'). The sentence has four clauses, each with a verb at its centre:

Main clause	Non-finite clause	Subordinate clause (with 'as')	Co-ordinate clause (with 'or')
The active little waders *feed* busily	*probing* this way and that	as they *wade* across shallow pools	or *follow* the tide line.

This economical and finely written sentence is able to show us several things going on at the same time: as the birds feed they wade and probe and follow the tide line.

ACTIVITY 4:

Write two or three parodies of the *Bird Guide* entries above describing the characteristic activities of a person engaged in a particular profession or occupation, such as a police-officer, a tennis-player, a bricklayer, a student or birdwatcher. Write the passages in three or four sentences and aim to use verbs in a varied and interesting way.

ACTIVITY 5:

Choose an essay you have written recently and identify all the full verbs in it. Write a short analysis of your choice of verbs in the essay – how well do they express what you were trying to say? Now, using a thesaurus, try to improve the effectiveness of the verbs by choosing substitutes for any in the original which you think could be improved. Provide a short commentary to explain some of your decisions.

Open word classes: the adverb

Adverbs are used to add to or modify the verb. They can also act as degree modifiers in front of adjectives: 'he was *very* cold'; 'she was *quite* interested'; 'I'm *nearly* ready', '*rather* shy'. The relationship between verbs and adverbs is similar to the one between nouns and adjectives. Adverbs give extra detail about the exact time, place or manner (the way something happens or is done) of the action or state we are expressing in the verb. For example:

> I kissed my mother *affectionately.*
> The wall *suddenly* collapsed.
> A perfect world has *never* existed.
> I will vacuum *soon.*
> I *always* sleep *well.*

Note that adverbs often, but not always, end in '–ly'. The above examples show the use of adverbs to express the *time* and *manner* of actions and states. Adverbs of *place* are harder to find in single word form; usually place is expressed by a group of words: for example, 'I'll see you *in the Market Square*'; 'I *always* walk *through the park on my way home*' (the frequency, place and time of the walking are expressed here).

> The black cat sits *on the mat.*
> The black cat sits *precariously.*
> The black cat sits *on the mat at noon everyday.*

Most adverbs do their work inside clauses, as above, but there are some which work across clauses, to express a logical link between them. These adverbs are very important in essay writing in which the links in the chain of an argument need to be indicated. For example:

> What we have just said is true as far as we are concerned. *However*, not everyone would agree with us.

Without 'however' there would be two separate ideas: 'however' links them. Other adverbs which work like this are:

> therefore, thus, first/secondly/thirdly, in other words, finally

What they all have in common is that they are inviting comparison between the meanings of the two verbs in the two clauses they link.

Adverbs in action

To show adverbs in action we will return to the poetic and economical piece of bird watching lore we examined earlier. Each of the verbs within it is carefully qualified by a high number of adverbials, one or two of which are expressed by single word adverbs, in order to show how and where, in what way and at what exact time the birds wade or probe or twist and turn. We have identified the adverbs in the passage in italic:

> Purple Gallinule: *Rather** shy, the Purple Gallinule spends much time *inside reedbeds* or, *in Africa, in papyrus swamps*, but also feeds *along the fringes*, walking *in and out of the vegetation / at any time of day. In the evening* it *often* clambers up stems of reeds or papyrus and sits up *in the open*, surveying the landscape.
>
> (Keith and Gooders 1980: 446)

> Dunlin: The active little waders feed *busily*, probing *this way and that* as they wade *across shallow pools* or follow the tide line. They *sometimes* gather *in immense numbers / at favoured feeding grounds* and will form dense packs *in flight*. They *alternately* show white, then dark, as they twist and turn *in unison in the air*.
>
> (Keith and Gooders 1980: 476)

As you can see, most single-word adverbs are easy to identify because they end in '–ly' ('busily', 'alternately'), but there are only two in this form, and apart from the other single words such as 'sometimes', the rest of the adverbials come in groups of words. Many of these adverbials are prepositional phrases (they begin with a preposition) such as 'in unison', 'in the air', 'at favoured feeding grounds', 'in flight', 'in the evening', 'up stems of reeds', 'inside reedbeds', 'in immense numbers'. Each of these prepositional

---

* Remember adverbs can be used as degree modifiers in front of adjectives as well and here the word 'rather' works to modify the degree of shyness of the birds: 'rather shy'.

phrases is acting as an adverbial because it is adding to the information we have about the verb – they tell us *how*, *where* and exactly *when* the gallinules are doing what gallinules do.

In the passage above there are two very similar clauses:

> … as they wade across shallow pools
> … as they twist and turn in unison in the air

Remember these are subordinate (dependent) clauses. They begin with a subordinating conjunction ('as') which means that they are dependent upon the main clause: 'The birds probe, *as* they wade'. 'As' clauses of this kind are acting as adverbial clauses of time.

ACTIVITY 6:

In the last chapter we showed you an extract from Elizabeth Bowen's short story 'Mysterious Kor' and we commented on the high number of adverbs and adverbials she had used in the piece to create certain effects. Write a short descriptive piece of your own on a subject of your choice, in the style of Elizabeth Bowen, using a high number of adverbials of different kinds in a variety of positions in the sentences. Comment on your passage, comparing it with the Bowen original.

This ends our presentation of the open word classes: nouns, adjectives, verbs and adverbs. Awareness of these classes is important because how writers, including you, use them can make a big difference to style and expression. We have already mentioned Hemingway's mistrust of adjectives and Conrad's passion for them. Imagine a piece of writing in which all the nouns were abstract, for example; or a piece of descriptive writing packed with adverbs of place and time; or writing in which all the verbs expressed states not actions. All such expressive differences, as part of the meaning and implication of writing, would need to be noted by you as a reader and a writer.

Closed word classes

We turn now to the closed word classes. These hardly ever change and they mostly express the logical links between our experiences of the world and the structures of language itself. Words like 'this', 'those', 'but', 'not', 'most', 'if' represent the closed word classes. Language cannot work without them, but you do not need to be quite so aware of most of them as you do the open word classes. This is because they do not usually play such a major part in creating style and implication as the open word classes do. But we say 'most of them': for essay writing, for example, an awareness of how the conjunctions work is important. We will present the closed word classes briefly.

Closed word classes: the conjunction

Conjunctions are used to join together words, phrases and clauses within sentences. We have already explained in Chapter 1 that conjunctions fall into two types and are sometimes called *connectives*, a word used to describe their function.

Type 1 (called coordinating conjunctions) has three main words in it: 'and', 'but' and 'or'. Type 2 (called subordinating conjunctions) is much larger, containing over forty commonly used words (like 'because', 'if', 'while', 'when', 'until', 'before', 'as well as') which would appear in a sentence in the following way: 'I'll stop *when* he does', or 'I won't stop *until* he does', or 'I'm not going to stop *before* he does'. In each case the conjunction joins the first and second parts of the sentence. To remind yourself you might want to look back at the table of subordinating conjunctions in Chapter 1 (p. 19).

> The black cat sits quietly on the big mat *and* considers the nature of her existence. (co-ordinating conjunction)
>
> The black cat sits quietly on the big mat *because* she is thinking about the nature of her existence. (subordinating conjunction)

Conjunctions in action

Conjunctions are very important in analytical and what we call expository writing (writing with an argument) because they are the words that act as connectors of the various parts of the argument.

ACTIVITY 7:

Write a short piece of expository writing (based on argument) on a controversial subject such as modern art or body piercing or a topic of your own choice using as many subordinating conjunctions from the list in Chapter 1 as you can. Comment briefly on your choice of conjunctions and their effectiveness in a short commentary.

Alternatively, identify the conjunctions in the essay you worked on in Activity 5 and analyse the effectiveness of your choices. Substitute with alternative conjunctions where you think you can make improvements and write a short commentary on what you have done and how you think you have improved the writing through your use of conjunctions.

Closed word classes: the pronoun

These are words that stand in for a noun or a noun phrase (hence pro-noun). Instead of saying 'Jim', or 'Sheila', or 'the M4' all the time, language allows us to say 'he', or 'she', or 'it'. These words are all pronouns.

> *He* sits on the black mat.
> *He* sits on *it*.

There are several groups of pronouns that we will simply list:

Personal pronouns	I, you, he, she, it, we, they
Reflexive pronouns	these end in '–self' or '–selves', e.g. myself, yourself, themselves etc.
Possessive pronouns	my/mine, your/yours, her/hers etc.
Relative pronouns	we have looked at these in relation to relative clauses in the last chapter: who, whom, whose, which, that
Interrogative pronouns	these are more or less the same words as for relative pronouns but are used to ask questions ('interrogative' means 'questioning'): who, whom, whose, which, what
Demonstrative pronouns	this/these, that/those, i.e. 'near' and 'distant'
Reciprocal pronouns	each other, one another, i.e. 'two-way'

Pronouns in action

If we return to a children's story used earlier in this book we can see that there are many pronouns used within it partly because there is so much dialogue used. We have highlighted the pronouns with italics:

One day in summer Frog was not feeling well. Toad said, 'Frog, *you* are looking quite green.' 'But *I* always look green,' said Frog. '*I* am a frog.' 'Today *you* look very green even for a frog', said Toad. 'Get into *my* bed and rest.'

Toad made Frog a cup of hot tea. Frog drank the tea, and then *he* said, 'Tell *me* a story while *I* am resting.' 'All right,' said Toad. 'Let *me* think of a story to tell *you*.' Toad thought and thought. But *he* could not think of a story to tell Frog.

'*I* will go out on the front porch and walk up and down,' said Toad. 'Perhaps that will help *me* to think of a story.' Toad walked up and down on the porch for a long time. But *he* could not think of a story to tell Frog.

(Lobel 1970: 16–20)

Closed word classes: the preposition

Prepositions are placed before a noun or noun phrase to describe how that thing, person, place or object stands in relation to something else. Prepositions indicate space and time and identify relations between groups of words. There are a large number of these. We will list a few and come back to this word class when we discuss phrase structure.

Single-word prepositions include:

> in, on, under, after, during, of, at, over, round, since, through, from, between, up, with

Multiple-word prepositions include:

> by means of, in accordance with, away from, out of, in spite of, on behalf of, because of, due to, ahead of, near to, as far as

> The black cat sits *under* the big mat *during* the storm.

Prepositions in action

Earlier we looked at the description of bird activity from *The Collins Bird Guide* in order to show the varied use of verbs and adverbials, many of which were in the form of prepositional phrases such as 'in the evening' and 'along the fringes'. These prepositional phrases served to indicate how, where and when the birds were wading or feeding. They work to locate the action, as adverbials do. We can tell they are prepositional phrases because they begin with a preposition. We have identified the prepositions in the following passage in italic:

> Purple Gallinule: Rather shy, the Purple Gallinule spends much time *inside* reedbeds or, *in* Africa, *in* papyrus swamps, but also feeds *along* the fringes, walking *in* and *out of* the vegetation *at* any time *of* day. *In* the evening it often clambers *up* stems *of* reeds or papyrus and sits *up in* the open, surveying the landscape.

(Keith and Gooders 1980: 446)

Closed word classes: the determiner

Determiner is a functional term which refers to a mixed bag of words which 'pin down' or 'determine' a noun. Determiners include: 'a/an', 'the', 'some', 'all', 'many', 'few'. They make an idea, thing or event we are expressing more, or less, specific: consider, for instance, the difference between '*a* man' and '*the* man'. We all use them naturally without having to think much about them. You could call them 'specifiers'.

> *The* black cat sits on *a* big mat.
> *Some* people don't like *the* cat on *the* mat.

Word classes: an overview

We have now identified and sketched the word classes of English. As we have said, some are more practically important than others when we are thinking about key aspects of style in texts we are either reading or writing. You now, nevertheless, have a fairly complete 'map' of the word class terrain, even if you will be drawn to some regions more than others.

ACTIVITY 8:

Identify as many word classes as you can in the following sentences. Here we are asking you not to find clauses or phrases as we do elsewhere in the book, but rather to categorise each separate word in the sentence according to the eight different word classes. Remember what we have said about word class versatility, i.e. that words can play more than one word class role. A dictionary might help with the word class of 'all' in the sixth example. Read carefully; good dictionaries are very informative.

> His European clothes were spotted immediately.
> The black dog ran quickly towards his owner.
> He always works quickly.
> The night was dark.
> The woman in black clothes walked carefully along the wall.
> Love conquers all.
> This stupendous fragmentariness heightened the dreamlike strangeness of her bridal life. (Eliot 1965: 224)

Here is the famous opening of George Orwell's futuristic novel *Nineteen Eighty-Four* (1949). Orwell, like Hemingway, favoured a plain, economical approach to words and sentences. Read the passage. Then with one colour pen underline the verbs in the passage. Using different colour pens for each word class underline nouns, adjectives and adverbs (or phrases performing an adverbial role). Write a brief analysis of 300–500 words, exploring the use of language in the passage as a whole and using what you have learnt in the chapter to comment on how Orwell achieves his effects through his use of particular word classes. If you try to classify every single word, the activity may become mechanical and you may lose a sense of the style and flow of the passage. So be careful and be practical: look at enough word classes to form an impression of Orwell's style.

> It was a bright cold day in April, and the clocks were striking thirteen. Winston Smith, his chin nuzzled into his breast in an effort to escape the vile wind, slipped quickly through the glass doors of Victory Mansions, though not quickly enough to prevent a swirl of gritty dust from entering along with him.
>
> The hallway smelt of boiled cabbage and old rag mats. At one end of it a coloured poster, too large for indoor display, had been tacked to the wall. It depicted simply an enormous face, more than a metre wide: the face of a man of about forty-five, with a heavy black moustache and ruggedly handsome features. Winston made for the stairs. It was no use trying the lift. Even at the best of times it was seldom working, and at present the electric current was cut off during daylight hours. It was part of the economy drive in preparation for Hate Week. The flat was seven flights up, and Winston, who was thirty-nine and had a varicose ulcer above his right ankle, went slowly, resting several times on the way. On each landing, opposite the lift-shaft, the poster with the enormous face gazed from the wall. It was one of those pictures which are so contrived that the eyes follow you about when you move. BIG BROTHER IS WATCHING YOU, the caption beneath it ran.
>
> Inside the flat a fruity voice was reading out a list of figures which had something to do with the production of pig-iron. The voice came from an oblong metal plaque like a dulled mirror which formed part of the surface of the right-hand wall. Winston turned a switch and the voice sank somewhat, though the words were still distinguishable. The instrument (the telescreen, it was called) could be dimmed, but there was no way of shutting it off completely.

(Orwell 1987: 3)

Different kinds of writing will inevitably require different proportions of certain word classes. We might say for instance that academic writing is likely to use a number of subordinating conjunctions. Strongly visual descriptive writing, such as that typified by the passage from Kingsley's *Alton Locke*, is likely to use a high number of adjectives and nouns, but when the author is trying to create an impression of movement, such as Bowen and the authors of the bird guide, then verbs, adverbs and prepositions will all be very important. Take two pieces of your own recent writing which contrast strongly in terms of genre and style (e.g. a short story and an essay, or a formal letter and a memo). Look closely at the word class choices you have made in each. Is there a preponderance of certain word classes? Why is this and is it appropriate to the form and function of the two pieces of writing? Write a short commentary comparing the two pieces of writing in terms of your choice of word classes in each.

Summary

In this chapter we have:

- identified and defined the eight principal word classes in English
- showed how each of these word classes create particular effects in writing.

References

Conrad, Joseph (1981) *Heart of Darkness* [1899]. Harmondsworth: Penguin.

Eliot, George (1965) *Middlemarch* [1871–72]. Harmondsworth: Penguin.

Hemingway, Ernest (1992) 'In Another Country' [1927] in David Lodge, *The Art of Fiction*. Harmondsworth: Penguin.

Keith, Stuart and Gooders, John (1980) *The Collins Bird Guide*. London: Collins.

Kingsley, Charles (1892) *Alton Locke: Tailor and Poet* [1850]. London: Macmillan.

Lobel, Arnold (1970) 'The Story' in *Frog and Toad are Friends*. London: Harper Collins Juvenile Books.

Orwell, George (1987) *Nineteen Eighty-Four* [1949]. Harmondsworth: Penguin.

Ruskin, John (1995) 'The Savageness of Gothic Architecture' in *The Stones of Venice* [1851–53]. London: Dent.

Phrase grammar

Rebecca Stott and Peter Chapman

Word classes and phrase classes

In the last chapter we showed you eight basic functions or jobs that words have in sentences, and we showed you, too, how words can move about between jobs like actors, assuming the role of an adjective in one sentence ('dusty'), a noun in another ('dust') or a verb ('dusted'). The adverb of dust would be 'dustily' and it does exist as a word but is rarely used. In our examples we have mainly used single words to illustrate the eight classes doing their eight different jobs; here is a sentence using all eight word classes:

Determiner	Adjective	Noun	Adverb	Verb
The	beautiful	sunshine	regularly	contributes

Preposition	Pronoun	Noun	Conjunction	Noun
to	our	well-being	and	happiness.

This sentence uses one word to play each of the word class roles. The role of noun is 'played' three times (once by a concrete noun, 'sunshine'; and twice by abstract nouns, 'well-being' and 'happiness'). Just pause for a moment and check this through.

However, being able to classify the words in a sentence in terms of word classes is only part of the picture. Such knowledge is only useful if it can enable you to understand the use of language in a particular passage and the ways in which sentence construction and syntax (the choice and order of elements in a clause) contribute to the effect of the passage. Classification is only useful as a tool for analysis and exploration. And this is where it begins to be possible to combine the grammatical knowledge we have presented so far in this book in such a way that it can be put to use in the detailed study of any kind of writing, literary and non-literary, and give you a sharper awareness of the writing structures you yourself use. The main function of this chapter is to introduce you to phrase structure, but we will also be looking for opportunities to put together what you have learnt about grammar and writing by looking at the concept of *syntax*, which is a useful term for describing the way words are arranged grammatically in sentences.

In the last chapter we showed you how to classify each word in clauses and sentences. This is called analysing the grammar of word classes. There is a second, related method of analysing the way words are put together and this looks, not at individual words, but rather at phrases or word clusters within the clause. We call this analysing the *phrase structure* of clauses. Neither way is better than the other – they are simply alternative methods of examining syntax. Sometimes one method will be more applicable than another, depending upon the writing you are exploring. We will give you examples of how the different approaches might be useful.

Sometimes words do act alone in expressing a clause element. For example:

Word class identification

Pronoun	Verb	Noun	Adverb	Conjunction	Pronoun	Verb	Noun
She	studied	grammar	yesterday	while	he	cooked	supper.

Clause element identification

She	studied	grammar	yesterday	while	he	cooked	supper.
Subject	Verb	Object	Adverbial	Connective	Subject	Verb	Object

But, just as often, possibly more often, single words do their work in groups of words called phrases which in turn express clause elements. Here is an example:

Noun phrase	Verb phrase	Noun phrase	Prepositional phrase
The guy next door	was studying	his new grammar book	in the garden.
Subject	**Verb**	**Object**	**Adverbial**

The term *phrase* means a cluster of two or more words in a sentence. It is different from a clause because it lacks the subject + verb structure which is essential to the clause. We shall identify five different kinds of phrase structure:

- noun phrase
- verb phrase
- adverbial phrase
- adjectival phrase
- prepositional phrase.

This means that when we change the focus from single words to phrases we are thinking about the arrangements of words, but not different basic functions. The other three categories – conjunctions, pronouns and determiners – do not make significant phrases, though they are, of course, significant word classes. This is because they are closed word classes and do not adapt or modify to the same degree as the other groups.

Identifying phrase classes

We must now make some comments on phrase identification, starting with what happens inside a phrase: does a noun phrase, for example, have to have only nouns in it? The answer is: no, it does not. Four of the five phrase types are (class) identified by the key or head word in them, but they can and do have other classes of words in them too. The task is to identify the head word and this does take a little practice. So let us start by going back to our sentence about 'sunshine'.

> The beautiful sunshine regularly contributes to our well-being and happiness.

ACTIVITY 1:

Earlier, we were thinking about the word class of each word, but now we would like you to find the phrase structure of this one-clause sentence. Can you find words working together here to form word groups? Write down your first thoughts in a sequence of boxes containing the groups of words or put circles around the groups you think belong in phrases or clusters.

Perception of phrasing is partly grammatical analysis and partly listening to 'the shape of the meaning'. For example, you might have grouped 'regularly' with 'contributes' or 'contributes to'; you might have grouped 'to' with 'our well-being and happiness'; and you might have separated 'our well-being' and 'happiness' – like this:

The beautiful sunshine	regularly contributes to	our well-being and happiness.
The beautiful sunshine	regularly contributes	to our well-being and happiness.
The beautiful sunshine	regularly contributes to	our well-being	and happiness.

The point we are making is that response to the phrasing of sentences, 'hearing' how the meaning is shaped, is a vital aspect of language awareness which we recommend that you consciously develop by reading and listening. You already have this skill as a reader and writer but the task is to make your ear more finely tuned to the syntax of sentences. Reading aloud is a critical skill here. What you learn about grammar and 'syntax' will contribute to your own perception of structure and meaning. Start by using your intuition and your 'inner ear' through reading aloud.

Here is how *we* would analyse the phrase structure of the sentence. It consists of a noun phrase, a single-word adverb, a verb phrase with a main verb and a verb particle (one of those little extra words, often prepositions, attached to verbs such as 'hung *over*' or 'call *on*'), and a second noun phrase with two key nouns, both of equal importance and so co-ordinated by 'and':

Noun phrase	Adverb	Verb phrase	Noun phrase
The beautiful sunshine	regularly	contributes to	our well-being and happiness.
Subject	Adverbial	Verb	Object

You should also be able to see from your work in Chapter 2 that each phrase expresses a clause element (here the subject, adverbial, verb and object). Now you could argue that 'regularly contributes to' is a separate unit or phrase by itself because the adverb 'regularly' seems to belong to the verb in a cluster of its own. There are a number of variations on phrase structure or word groupings which you can argue for depending upon your sense of the internal structure of the sentence, but it isn't a question of anything goes, however. You would find it very difficult to argue for the following phrase structure because the words don't cluster grammatically or logically together:

| The beautiful | sunshine contributes | regularly to our well-being and happiness. |

Having demonstrated the basic principles of phrase structure, we will now look at each of the phrase types one by one.

Noun phrases

Noun phrases can be brief and simple but they can also be extended and complex – much more so than other phrase classes. The grammatical features of noun phrases are as follows.

- Noun phrases express the subject and object functions in clauses (as do single nouns and pronouns). They can also express the complement function of 'to be' (e.g. 'She is *a well-respected doctor*').
- Noun phrases are extremely variable in length.
- Noun phrases have a noun as the head word.

Noun phrases typically contain other word classes: 'the beautiful sunshine' contains a determiner ('the') and an adjective ('beautiful'), for instance, as well as a noun, ('sunshine'), but the noun 'sunshine' forms the head word and it does a noun's job of labelling a concrete thing or abstract concept. Noun phrases quite often contain a large number of words clustered around a head word. This can be illustrated by building up a noun phrase from one word to several, as follows:

Noun phrase with head noun in italic	Verb	Adjective
Cakes	taste	nice.
The *cakes*	taste	nice.
All the *cakes*	taste	nice.
All the iced *cakes*	taste	nice.
All the iced *cakes* in the window	taste	nice.
All the iced *cakes* and all the *eclairs* and the chocolate *buns* on the plate in the window	taste	nice.

So, a noun can stand alone or be accompanied by a cluster of other words in front of it and/or after it. If we were to break down the noun phrase 'All the iced cakes in the window' into word classes it would look like this:

Determiner	Determiner	Adjective	Head noun	Preposition	Determiner	Noun
All	the	iced	cakes	in	the	window

The head word is the noun 'cakes'. All the other words add extra details about the head word and idea of the whole phrase.

Here are some further examples of noun phrases identified in italic:

> *The black dog* chewed *the long, yellow rug.*
> *The man wearing the sinister overcoat* ran *a hundred desperate yards.*

Sometimes identifying phrase structure is very useful because identifying noun phrases rather than individual nouns helps us to see the structural pattern of the sentence more clearly – particularly in sentences with complex noun phrases in them. Here is an example of what we mean by a complex noun phrase:

> That man standing in the road who became angry because you made a face at him as you walked past is Detective-Constable Philips of Scotland Yard.

We have said that the subject of the clause is often expressed by a noun phrase. So in the above sentence which is the subject noun phrase? And which is the head word?

The subject noun phrase is very long and made up of several parts. It looks like this:

> That man standing in the road who became angry because you made a face at him as you walked past

The head word of this long subject noun phrase is 'man'. The verb is 'is' (present tense of the linking verb 'to be'), which follows immediately at the end of the subject noun phrase. The rest of the sentence consists of another noun phrase ('Detective-Constable Philips of Scotland Yard'), which is acting as a subject complement.

But if all this is so, then it means that *whole clauses can be embedded in noun phrases*. In this sentence the noun phrase includes:

- a non-finite clause ('standing in the road')
- a relative clause ('who became angry') and
- two subordinate clauses: ('when you walked past') and ('because you made a face at him').

When a noun phrase is as complex as this, it can be subdivided for easier analysis and understanding. It can usefully be divided into three parts:

Pre-modification	Words coming *before* the head noun – usually determiners and adjectives
Head noun	The main noun in the noun phrase
Post-modification	Words coming *after* the head noun, usually • prepositional phrases (e.g. 'the man *in the road*') • finite clauses (e.g. 'that man *who is angry*') • non-finite clauses (e.g. 'the man *running* away') • adverbials (e.g. 'the man *over there*') • adjectives (e.g. 'the man, *tired and old*')

We have been using the terms 'modify' and 'modification' throughout this book (adjectives modify nouns, adverbs modify verbs) so it should be easier to see what these apparently extremely technical terms mean. 'Pre-modify', 'pre-modifiers' and 'pre-modification' simply refer to what comes *before* the head noun (the prefix 'pre' means 'before'); post-modification refers to what comes *after* the head noun to complete the meaning of the noun phrase (the prefix 'post' means 'after'). To return to the sentence above, you will see that it has one pre-modifying word ('That') and eighteen words of post-modification.

ACTIVITY 2:

Here are some examples of sentences with complex subject noun phrases. Identify the subject noun phrase in each example and then work out the number of words acting as pre-modifiers and those acting as post-modifiers in the noun phrase. Only one of the sentences contains post-modification. If there are clauses in the noun phrase such as relative clauses or non-finite clauses identify these. There may be other noun phrases in each sentence but your task is to find the noun phrase which is acting as the subject.

> A totally uniform, regionally neutral, and unarguably prestigious variety does not yet exist worldwide. (Crystal 1996: 14)
> Some other regional grammatical variants are mentioned later in the book. (Crystal 1996: 22)
> The ideal which Kipling's verse disseminated across the globe was of Empire as a school of practical skills and unrewarded duty. (Boehmer 1995: 52)

ACTIVITY 3:

Here is part of the passage from Kingsley's *Alton Locke* that we looked at in the last chapter in relation to nouns and adjectives. There are eight noun phrases in the passage, two embedded in prepositional phrases acting as adverbials, two in the subject position. Identify and label these eight noun phrases. Count the number of pre- and post-modifying words in each and identify the head word and the clause function of each:

> From the butchers' and greengrocers' shops the gaslights flared and flickered, wild and ghastly, over haggard groups of slipshod dirty women, bargaining for stale meat and frost-bitten vegetables, wrangling about short weight and bad quality. Fish stalls and fruit stalls lined the edge of the greasy pavement, sending up odours as foul as the language of sellers and buyers.
>
> (Kingsley 1892: 66)

Before we move away from noun phrases, here is a wonderful example of the use of a series of beautifully crafted noun phrases in a stanza from a poem in Seamus Heaney's collection *Station Island*, called 'Old Pewter'. Here Heaney is reflecting on 'what the soul's composed of' (perhaps there is a slight ironic echo of 'what are little girls made of?').

> Glimmerings are what the soul's composed of.
> Fogged-up challenges, far conscience-glitters
> And hang-dog, half-truth earnests of true love.
> And a whole late-flooding thaw of ancestors.
>
> (Heaney 1984: 22)

Instead of beginning 'The soul is composed of . . .' and then listing the qualities and images that make up the soul, Heaney plays with the word order so that he can begin with the powerful word 'glimmerings'. This is an unusual noun, derived from the verb 'to glimmer'. Each of the noun phrases that almost entirely fill the rest of the stanza is both extraordinarily elusive and suggestive. Heaney uses unusual combinations of words as compound nouns or adjectives (words joined by a hyphen such as the adjective 'fogged-up' and the noun 'conscience-glitters') to form new concepts such as 'fogged-up challenges'.

ACTIVITY 4:

Identify four unusual noun phrases in the poem and explain what you think Heaney means by each one. What is 'a fogged-up challenge' or a 'far conscience-glitter'? And what does Heaney mean, for instance, when he says that the soul is composed of 'a whole late-flooding thaw of ancestors'?

Adjectival phrases

Love them (like Conrad) or hate them (like Hemingway), adjectives are the largest word class after nouns and verbs. In Chapter 3 we showed you how adjectives can come both before nouns ('dusty road') or after nouns ('the road, dusty and pot-holed') or both before and after the noun ('the long road, dusty from the heat'). We also told you that adjectives can also come after linking verbs and act as subject complements ('the road was dry and dusty'). In looking at noun phrases we also showed you that many of them are made up of nouns and accompanying adjectives.

There are three kinds of adjectival clusters you need to be aware of. The first is simply a string of adjectives, two or more, in front of a noun, as in: 'the *long, dusty* road' or 'the *beautiful, little, green, Indian* rug'. In these examples the strings of adjectives are contributing to noun phrases, so they are not adjectival phrases strictly speaking but just sequences of the same word class within a noun phrase.

The second kind of adjectival cluster is a genuine adjectival phrase because it has a head word which is an adjective but also another word in front of the adjective which is not. For example in the following three sentences we've put the adjectival phrase in italic and picked out the main adjective within the adjectival phrase in capital letters:

> That is *very NICE.*
> I'm *pretty SURE* I'm right.
> You're *quite WET.*

Words which add extra meaning to the adjective like this ('very', 'pretty', 'quite') are called functionally *degree modifiers* (and they are in fact adverbs if they were categorised in terms of word class): they change the degree (amount) of 'niceness' or 'rightness' or 'wetness'. Other degree modifiers are: 'rather', 'somewhat', 'more' and 'too'.

The third kind of adjectival phrase is formed by using an adjective after a linking verb (such as 'to be', 'to seem', 'to look') and then expanding the meaning of the adjective. Note that the adjective is the head word in the following italic phrases:

> She is *CLEVER enough to go.*
> Your home is *LARGER than mine.*
> He seems *PROUD of his children.*
> The monster looked *BIG and GREEN.*

Many similes are made up of adjectival phrases of this kind. Think of the following: 'bright as a button', 'quiet as a mouse', 'silent as the grave', 'deaf as a doorpost', 'cool as a cucumber'.

ACTIVITY 5:

Write a poem about a person you know which is made up primarily of a combination of adjectives and adjectival phrases. Here's one we wrote about a little girl called Hannah who is six years old.

> *White blonde* your hair is,
> *As bright as the sun*
> And the garden they have planted you
> Is *full of sunflowers.*
> *Sweet-tempered* yet *quick to cry*
> Born in April –
> *As changeable as an April day*
> And *as promising.*

ACTIVITY 6:

Find three or four adverts from a magazine or newspaper and compare the way they use adjectives and adjectival phrases to describe their products. Write up your analysis in the form of a short report.

Verb phrases

The verb function in a clause can be one word or several, as we have already mentioned. Unlike the noun phrase, however, all the words in verb phrases are verb forms of one kind or another even though the main verb or base verb is like a head noun. There are, though, a large number of different verb forms and functions, and we must sketch these in here. We shall choose a verb, more or less at random, and show all the forms it can take. The verb 'to sing' can have the following appearances in sentences. When we are talking about verbs, and perhaps listing them, we usually refer to them by the 'to' form, as here. We have highlighted the verb phrases in italic for clarity.

Verb phrase	Time implication
I *sing* in the shower.	Every time
I *am singing* in the shower.	Present moment
I *sang* three songs in the shower.	Past
I *have sung* songs all my life.	Past up to the present moment
I *am going to sing* a song at your wedding.	'Going to' expresses future meaning
I *had been singing* for several seconds when the curtain came up.	Two related events in the past
I *may sing* for you.	Possibility
I *should not sing* so much.	Obligation
I *wanted to sing* for her.	An example of two main verbs together, the second in the 'to' form

Regular and irregular verbs

Note that with most verbs we simply add '–ed' to make the past tense (look/ed, walk/ed, search/ed), but many need to be changed in different ways to make the past tense (sing/sang, run/ran, see/saw, is/was). We call such verbs 'irregular'. Small children learn about making the past tense through adding '–ed' first of all and this can lead to some interesting variations in irregular verbs; a child may sometimes say 'I singed the song' or 'I runned to school', for instance.

The auxiliary plus main verb structure

You can see from the above chart that verb phrases are generally much less variable than noun phrases in that they are usually made up of a main verb accompanied by up to three (and very rarely four) auxiliaries. Auxiliary verbs, or 'auxiliaries' as they are called, assist the main verb in a clause or phrase to express several basic grammatical contrasts in number, tense, person or modality. Here are some examples:

Auxiliary verbs	Main verb
	cooks
is	cooking
has been	cooking
must have been	cooking
(rare) must have been being	cooked

Usually you will find all the parts of a verb phrase together, such as 'must have been cooking', but sometimes writers will fragment the parts of the verb phrase in order to achieve a particular effect. We will look at an example of this later in the chapter when we look at a poem by Gerard Manley Hopkins. A simple but rather awkward example might be: 'He must, we suppose, have been cooking'. The American nineteenth-century novelist Mark Twain once humorously complained about the way in which the verb phrase is often fragmented in the German language:

> A verb has a hard enough time of it in this world when it is all together. It's downright inhuman to split it up. But that's what those Germans do. They take part of a verb and put it down here, like a stake, and they take the other part of it and put it a way over yonder like another stake, and between these two limits they just shovel in German.
>
> (Twain 1910: 54)

Sentences which have unusual syntax can be awkward and confusing or very effective. It all depends upon the skill and control of the writer.

We have said that verb phrases are likely to be made up of a restricted number of words (verb plus up to four auxiliaries) and are therefore much more limited in their form than the almost unbounded extensions of the noun phrase. Once again, the advantage of being able to see sentences in terms of clusters or phrases of this kind is that it enables the reader to pick up the meaning more quickly. When sentences are long and intricate it helps to find the subject (often made up of a noun phrase) and its accompanying main verb or verb phrase.

ACTIVITY 7:

Here is a long and complex sentence from George Eliot's *The Mill on the Floss* (1860). The sentence describes a boy, Tom Tulliver, who has dressed up as a pirate for a theatrical event. He has used a burnt cork as face-paint to draw on a pair of black eyebrows and a beard in an effort to make himself look fierce. Find the main clause or clauses in this passage and then identify the subject and verb phrases in the main clause or clauses. When you have done this, try to rewrite the sentence by shortening and clarifying it.

> Dissatisfied with the pacific aspect of a face which had no more than the faintest hint of flaxen eyebrow, together with a pair of amiable blue-grey eyes and round pink cheeks that refused to look formidable let him frown as he would before the looking-glass ... he had had recourse to that unfailing source of the terrible burnt cork, and had made himself a pair of black eyebrows that met in a satisfactory manner over his nose and were matched by a less carefully adjusted blackness about the chin.
>
> (Eliot 1979: 254)

Adverbial phrases

Single-word adverbs with a '–ly' ending such as 'quickly' or 'silently' are common, but phrases are not unknown, for example when the adverb is accompanied by an degree modifier: 'quite often', 'very slowly'. There can be several in a sentence: 'I *quite often* cycle to work *very slowly*'. In this sentence the verb is 'to cycle'; the first adverbial phrase tells you the *frequency* of the cycling; and the second tells you the *manner* of the cycling.

ACTIVITY 8:

The following phrases are either adjectival phrases or adverbial phrases. Identify which is which. The easiest way to do it is to find the head word in each phrase and decide whether this is acting as an adjective or adverb.

> not too awkward
> terribly slowly
> easy to please
> quick to judge
> quite sharply
> very quickly indeed

Prepositional phrases

We have already introduced you to prepositional phrases with an adverbial function in Chapters 2 and 3. Prepositional phrases are usually easy to identify because they begin with a preposition: '*in* the back garden'; '*underneath* the bed'; '*across* the mountain'; '*due to* the awful weather'; '*ahead of* the queue'; '*on top of* the CD player'; '*in accordance with* your recent request'. Notice that the preposition itself can be expressed in one, two or three words, as in the above examples.

Prepositional phrases can often be found within complex noun phrases in the postmodifying position, as you can see in the following examples (we have identified the noun phrase in italic and capitalised the part of it which is a prepositional phrase):

> I want to have *a party FOR ALL MY FRIENDS.*
> I saw *a man IN A RAINCOAT.*
> *The iced cakes IN THE WINDOW* taste nice.

In the above examples, the prepositional phrases all contribute to the noun phrase. Another way of describing them would be to say that they function as adjectivals. But not all prepositional phrases do this. Look, for instance, at this sentence from Elizabeth Bowen's 'Mysterious Kor':

> *From the promontory of the pavement outside the gates* you saw *at once up the road and down the street: from behind where you stood, between the gate-posts,* appeared the lesser strangeness of grass and water and trees.

(Bowen 1987: 32)

Here, and in many other sentences, the prepositional phrases function as adverbials in the sense that they add information to the verb about time, place and manner. In the following examples, for instance, the prepositional phrases are all functioning as adverbials:

> *In the morning*, we went home.   (time)
> The car came racing *down the road*.   (place)
> He responded with a *malicious grin*.   (manner)

So if you are faced with prepositional phrases functioning as adjectivals or adverbials what do we call them? The answer is that it depends upon what kind of analysis you are doing and your judgement of the structure of the sentence. As a rule it is usually better to call them 'prepositional phrases' but you might also want to point out their function.

ACTIVITY 9:

Identify the prepositional phrases in the following sentence from Thomas Hardy's *Tess of the D'Urbervilles* (1891):

> In these long June days the milkmaids, and, indeed, most of the household, went to bed at sunset or sooner, the morning work before milking being so early and heavy at a time of full pails.

(Hardy 1965: 159)

ACTIVITY 10:

We are now ready to look at a longer passage, this time from Hardy's *The Return of the Native* (1878). Use the knowledge you have acquired about both word classes and phrase structure to explore the use of language in the passage; think also about the positioning of words and phrases in sentences. There is no need to analyse every sentence. You might choose five sentences which catch your attention to write out and analyse in detail, for instance. We have stressed the importance of judgement and a good ear for finding phrase structure. Begin by reading the passage aloud several times to get a feel for the structure. Write up your observations in the form of a short essay on the passage.

Along the road walked an old man. He was white-headed as a mountain, bowed in the shoulders, and faded in general aspect. He wore a glazed hat, an ancient boat-cloak, and shoes; his brass buttons bearing an anchor upon their face. In his hand was a silver-headed walking-stick, which he used as a veritable third leg, perseveringly dotting the ground with its point at every few inches' interval. One would have said that he had been, in his day, a naval officer of some sort or other.

Before him stretched the long, laborious road, dry, empty, and white. It was quite open to the heath on each side, and bisected that vast dark surface like the parting-line on a head of black hair, diminishing and bending away on the furthest horizon.

The old man frequently stretched his eyes ahead to gaze over the tract that he had yet to traverse. At length he discerned, a long distance in front of him, a moving spot, which appeared to be a vehicle, and it proved to be going the same way as that in which he himself was journeying. It was the single atom of life that the scene contained, and it only served to render the general loneliness more evident. Its rate of advance was slow, and the old man gained upon it sensibly.

When he drew nearer he perceived it to be a spring van, ordinary in shape, but singular in colour, this being a lurid red. The driver walked beside it; and, like his van, he was completely red. One dye of that tincture covered his clothes, the cap upon his head, his boots, his face, and his hands. He was not temporarily overlaid with the colour: it permeated him.

The old man knew the meaning of this. The traveller with the cart was a reddleman – a person whose vocation it was to supply farmers with redding for their sheep. He was one of a class rapidly becoming extinct in Wessex, filling at present in the rural world the place which, during the last century, the dodo occupied in the world of animals. He is a curious, interesting, and nearly perished link between obsolete forms of life and those which generally prevail.

(Hardy 1974: 37–8)

ACTIVITY 11:

Here is a list of book titles, band, film and product names formed by phrases. When phrases are used as titles in this way, disconnected from a sentence, it is sometimes difficult to decide what kind of phrase they form: e.g. adverbial, prepositional, noun, verb, adjectival. Try to identify the phrase classes in each case and list those titles which are difficult to identify. In some cases it will be easier to use word classes rather than phrase structure to examine the title. Try to explain why difficulties occur and identify ambiguities and possible meanings and implications.

War and Peace
Spice Girls
Much Ado About Nothing
Sexing the Cherry
Truly, Madly, Deeply
From Russia with Love
The Nun's Priest's Tale
The Mill on the Floss

Now try to find other titles of books, films, bands or products to lengthen the list for each group so that you have at least five for each group. Is it easier to find examples for some groups and not for others? Why is this?

Unravelling syntax

What do we mean by syntax? We described this word earlier as meaning simply sentence structure or the grammatical arrangement of words in a sentence. When essay markers comment on syntactical errors they usually mean that the student in question has written a number of sentences in which the word order or phrase structure is awkward to read or presents grammatical problems. At the same time many writers deliberately play with their readers' expectations of syntactical order in order to achieve certain effects. Writers of speeches also play around with word order in order to increase the emphasis on particular parts of the sentence. Like George Eliot, they might want us to take on board a number of qualifying phrases and clauses before we reach the main clause and the main verb. In other cases poets manipulate syntax in order to emphasise certain words or to create a particular rhythm or simply to produce new meanings and sounds through the careful disordering of common syntactical structures. One particular example of this is where the writer delays the main verb of the main clause to the end of the sentence, thus separating the subject and the verb by some distance in the sentence structure. This is called a *periodic sentence*.

The periodic sentence

This is a good example of how flexible the manipulation of structure can be, especially for the creation of particular effects. The following periodic sentence creates a big gap between the subject and the verb, so that the sentence is not completed for a very long time. It is from a speech made by the politician Robin Cook in 1991:

> Anybody who looks at the number of people on the waiting list, looks at the number of operations that are cancelled, looks at the pressure within the hospital situation, anybody that has been in one of the major hospitals recently knows that it is underfunded, even if they don't know by quite how much.

(Cambridge Evening News, 21 October 1991: 4)

This is a complicated sentence. The subject is 'anybody' followed by a number of relative clauses to form a list of observations about the National Health Service (NHS):

> Anybody who looks at the number of people on the waiting list
> (anybody) who looks at the number of operations that are cancelled
> (anybody) who looks at the pressure within the hospital situation
> (anybody) who has been in one of the major hospitals recently

Then comes the main verb 'knows'. All these people (and by now the group has swollen to a very large size) know what? They know that the NHS is underfunded. Robin Cook wants us to believe that this knowledge is not just his opinion or that of the Labour Party, it is common knowledge, held by the people – anybody knows that it is underfunded. And then he adds one final clause: 'even if they don't know by quite how much'. He knows this information, of course, and it is this special knowledge about how much that will enable him to act for the people. He has used the delayed verb for emphasis: to underline that his knowledge is common knowledge. He could have said 'everybody knows the NHS is underfunded' but, by using 'anybody' as his subject with four relative clauses attached to it before he stresses the verb 'knows', he can define exactly who does know this and, in his opinion, that includes all those people who use the NHS. He has used the periodic sentence to create a powerful rhetorical effect.

Poetic manipulations

Many poets working within tight metrical structures need to change the word order to maintain a rhythm or to create emphasis. Gerard Manley Hopkins wrote a series of sonnets at the end of the nineteenth century about his struggles with God and with his own faith called the 'Desolation Sonnets'. Hopkins uses a twisted and tortured syntax within a very tight verse form, the sonnet, to convey something of his own inner torture and self-loathing. Hopkins's work was not published until 1918, partly because of its subject matter and partly because of the difficulty readers had in comprehending his poems because of the complex syntax he used in them. Here is one of the 'Desolation Sonnets', written in 1885:

> No worst, there is none. Pitched past pitch of grief,
> More pangs will, schooled at forepangs, wilder wring.
> Comforter, where, where is your comforting?
> Mary, mother of us, where is your relief?
> My cries heave, herds-long; huddle in a main, a chief-
> Woe, world-sorrow; on an age-old anvil wince and sing –
> Then lull, then leave off. Fury had shrieked 'No ling
> Ering! Let me be fell: force I must be brief.'
> O the mind, mind has mountains; cliffs of fall
> Frightful, sheer, no-man-fathomed. Hold them cheap
> May who ne'er hung there. Nor does our small
> Durance deal with that steep nor deep. Here! Creep,
> Wretch, under a comfort serves in a whirlwind: all
> Life death does end and each day dies with sleep.

> (Hopkins 1987: 428)

We cannot do justice to such a complex and powerful poem in a few short lines, a poem which has taxed critics and philosophers and theologians for decades, but what we can claim is that what you have learnt so far in this book should stand you in good stead to at least begin to work out the puzzle that is this sonnet. Being able to identify phrase structure, knowing how to find the subject and main verb of a particular clause, these are the tools that you will need to use to try to grasp the syntax and the riddle of the poem's meaning. Most readers find that, however well they know the poem, each time they reread it they have to try to understand it again, even perhaps translate it, unravel it, put it into simpler syntactical structures, before they can then begin to ask why Hopkins says it all in this way.

We cannot go through the whole poem here but we will take a couple of Hopkins's sentences to show you how someone might go about unravelling the syntax:

> No worst, there is none.

The opening sentence, 'No worst, there is none', might be understood as 'There is nothing worse than this', but by writing it this way Hopkins emphasises the negative and metrically powerful 'No worst' at the beginning of the sentence. Here is another example:

> Pitched past pitch of grief,
> More pangs will, schooled at forepangs, wilder wring.

What is the main verb in this complicated structure? Try to follow our reasoning carefully and slowly here. The first verb of the sentence 'pitched' is a non-finite verb in a non-finite clause (remember '–ed' and '–ing' endings in which the non-finite verb is not made finite by tense, person or number). The word 'schooled' later in the sentence is also a non-finite verb. You can tell this in part because of the punctuation, which cordons off the two clauses, showing us that they are subordinate to the main clause. The main verb is actually 'wring', which comes right at the end of the sentence and second line. ('Wring' is an interesting choice of word here, because although it means 'to wring something out' or to 'wring' one's hands, it also sounds like 'ring' and there are other words in the sentence that suggest musical sounds such as 'pitch'. To wring wildly also suggests 'to ring bells wildly'.) The verb 'wring' is accompanied by an auxiliary 'will', from which it has been separated; it is very unusual for the verb phrase to be fragmented in this way in the English language and the reader has to reconnect them in order to make any sense. The auxiliary 'will' and the main verb 'wring' have also been separated by a non-finite clause ('schooled at forepangs') and an adjective 'wilder' which is actually working here as an adverb (Hopkins seems to mean 'more wildly wring' or 'wring more wildly'). So what is the subject of the main verb 'wring'? What is doing the wringing and who or what is being wrung? The subject is pangs ('pangs wring') and there is no object named (pangs wring what?), but we assume from the poem that Hopkins means that the pangs (pains) are wringing him almost as if he were being wrung out like a cloth or even being tortured (and there's the secondary suggestion of 'ringing' too).

So the clause structure looks like this:

Subject	Verb	Adverb
pangs	will wring	more wildly

In other words: there is more pain to come. Looking back at the whole sentence we can now see that Hopkins means something like the following:

> When the pain seems as if it can get no worse because it has passed the pitch of the most extreme form of suffering, sometimes more pain comes which, intensified by the first pain, wrings me even more wildly to even greater heights of pain.

What such an unravelling shows is the extraordinary compression of Hopkins's writing. We have added more than five times as many words (forty-four in total) in order to try to simplify Hopkins's original thirteen words! We have also had to restructure or reassemble it to grasp the meaning. This is all part of the experience and the enigma of Hopkins's writing and testifies to the spiritual and emotional complexity of his subject matter.

ACTIVITY 12:

Take two or three of the sentences from Hopkins's poem and, by adding words and rearranging the structure as we have done, try to rearrange the sentences into a more conventional and easy-to-read syntactical structure. Then compare the sentences with their originals and see what you have lost or gained in the simplification (sound, rhythm, juxtaposition of certain words, for instance).

ACTIVITY 13:

Find a piece of prose or poetry which you feel manipulates syntax in interesting and effective ways. Write a short commentary on how the writer has created certain effects through syntactical structures.

Summary

The key words and concepts we have used in this chapter are:

- phrase structure
- noun phrases
- adjectival phrases
- verb phrases
- adverbial phrases
- prepositional phrases
- syntax and its manipulation.

References

Boehmer, E. (1995) *Colonial and Postcolonial Literature*. Oxford: Oxford University Press.

Bowen, Elizabeth (1987) 'Mysterious Kor' [1946] in Malcolm Bradbury (ed.), *The Penguin Book of Short Stories*. Harmondsworth: Penguin.

Crystal, David (1996) *Rediscover Grammar*. Harlow: Longman.

Eliot, George (1979) *The Mill on the Floss* [1860]. Harmondsworth: Penguin.

Hardy, Thomas (1965) *Tess of the D'Urbervilles* [1891]. Basingstoke: Macmillan.

Hardy, Thomas (1974) *The Return of the Native* [1878] Basingstoke: Macmillan.

Heaney, Seamus (1984) *Station Island*. London: Faber and Faber.

Hopkins, Gerard Manley (1987) 'No Worst there Is None' [1885] in Christopher Ricks (ed.), *The New Oxford Book of Victorian Verse*. Oxford: Oxford University Press.

Kingsley, Charles (1892) *Alton Locke: Tailor and Poet* [1850]. London: Macmillan.

Twain, Mark (1910) 'The Disappearance of Literature' [1900] in *Mark Twain's Speeches*. New York: Harper and Brothers.

Punctuation

Rebecca Stott and Peter Chapman

The writer Isaac Babel once claimed: 'No iron can pierce the heart with such force as a full-stop put just at the right place'. Punctuation is not only an essential part of all forms of written communication from academic essays to letters accompanying job applications, but it can also achieve powerful stylistic effects if used well. All writers need to be able to understand the conventions of punctuation use if they are to write effectively. The following pages contain material which is designed to help you do this.

The system of punctuation we use today has evolved over many centuries. The Greek language was originally written without word boundaries and without any punctuation so that a written text was a solid block of symbols with no gaps between words, arranged across the page from the left to the right and then from the right back again, in a kind of zigzag. The first punctuation marks were introduced to help orators judge where to make a pause in the speech at a time when speaking aloud was an important public event. It wasn't until the advent of printing in the fifteenth century that punctuation began to be standardized, but even so, punctuation conventions have never been as rule-governed or consistent as the conventions of spelling. Authors of the same historical period, like Charles Dickens and George Eliot, often use different conventions of punctuation, and even today some aspects of punctuation remain, to a certain extent, a matter of personal judgement. There are also some differences between the American punctuation system and the English punctuation system which, though only slight, are crucial for editors and proof-readers, for instance, who are responsible for the typesetting of books that are published in both countries.

Punctuation is a means of marking boundaries and relationships between the different parts of written texts. The primary purposes of punctuation are:

- to create coherence in long stretches of writing by assisting the reader in seeing the grammatical structure of sentences: for instance, full stops mark the end of sentences; commas, colons and semi-colons indicate the clause and phrase structure within the sentence
- to signal to the reader how a piece of writing can be read aloud by using such marks or signals as exclamation marks, parentheses and question marks, for instance.

In this chapter we will be talking about both the *rules* and the *conventions* of punctuation because it is important to be able to distinguish between the two. For instance, we all put capital letters at the beginning of sentences and full stops at the end: thus we would call this a rule, not a convention. Likewise, we know that all questions should be followed by a question mark, so this would also be a rule. But there are also punctuation uses that are a matter of choice and convention. We would not all choose to put an exclamation mark at the end of the sentence 'Come over here', for instance, because it would depend on its context and on how we wanted it to sound. However, we should not think of punctuation use as being either a rule or a convention (compulsory or optional) but rather think in terms of a spectrum with absolute rules at one end and optional conventions at the other. The comma, for instance, is sometimes essential and sometimes optional depending on the particular sentence and combination of words.

Punctuation, as a system, clarifies grammatical structure and underlines meaning. We shall not give equal space to all parts of this system. Instead we will focus on a small group of punctuation marks – the ones that tend to cause problems for writers. This will mean spending a good deal of time examining the semi-colon, the colon, the comma and the apostrophe in particular.

But, before we show you the full punctuation system in the form of a table, first a word about the kind of examples we will use in the chapter to illustrate punctuation in use. Many school grammar books, particularly those written in the 1960s, used made-up examples which are drawn from a world where the girls are called Susan and the boys are called Peter, sentences which are full of dogs, balls, shopping, trees and cricket matches. We have tried instead to make up sentences that are a little more modern and to use actual examples from published literary and non-literary writing where we can. This is important because one of the best ways to learn about punctuation rules and conventions is to keep an eye on how they are used in everything that you read, particularly if there are one or two punctuation marks (like the semi-colon, for instance) which you are uncertain about. Many readers will find that they are familiar with most of the conventions; some readers will be uncertain about many. There are few writers, however, who can afford to be complacent about punctuation use as it is so central a part of sentence construction.

The punctuation system	
Full stop or point (.) (also called a 'period' in American English)	• Used to identify the end of a sentence • Used to indicate an abbreviation (B.C.) • Used within times, numbers and dates (4.25 p.m., £3.50) • Used in groups of three (an ellipsis) to show where a word or words have been left out (e.g. 'The Greek language was originally written ... with no gaps between words')
Semi-colon (;)	• Used to indicate the break between two equal, co-ordinate clauses in a sentence; it does similar work to the conjunction 'and' (e.g. 'The man in the trench-coat walked towards him; he was carrying a briefcase close to his chest') • Used to separate the complex parts of a list in partnership with a colon (e.g. 'Members of the department who share this responsibility are: Rebecca Stott, Head of Department; Peter Cattermole, Field Leader; David Booy, Academic Advisor; and Nigel Wheale, Academic Advisor')
Comma (,)	Many uses – but the main ones are: • to mark out the relationship between independent and dependent clauses (e.g. 'While he waited in the shop, she robbed the safe') • to show that one clause in a sentence is being used inside another such as a relative clause (e.g. 'Kevin Jones, *who disliked garlic as a boy*, found he couldn't live without it'), or an introductory phrase or clause (e.g. '*Having disliked garlic as a boy*, Kevin found he couldn't live without it') • to mark a run or list of similar grammatical units (words, phrases, clauses) (e.g. 'the park, the sky, the clouds' or 'Stella, light of my life, fire of my heart')
Colon (:)	• Used mainly to show that what follows is an explanation or amplification of what comes before it (e.g. 'Simeon begins with a confession: he claims he is not the author of the book') • Used to introduce examples and quotations (e.g. 'Simeon said: "I am not the author of this book"')

The punctuation system

Brackets ( )	• Used as an alternative to commas, marking the beginning and end of a separate unit within the sentence (e.g. 'Some writers (such as Dickens and Wordsworth) use a different system of notation')
Inverted commas or quotation marks – can be double or single (' ' " ")	Conventions of use vary. • used to indicate the beginning and end of speech or quotation within a text • also used to indicate speech within speech • used to indicate technical terms (e.g. 'This is known as "rhetoric"') • used to indicate ironic use of word (e.g. 'Only "nice" people use that word')
Hyphen (-)	• Used to join the two parts of a compound word (e.g. 'word-choice' or 'sky-blue' or 'Rhys-Jones')
Dash (longer than a hyphen) (–)	• Used to indicate a summarising comment at the end of a sentence (e.g. 'The strikers included plumbers, electricians, carpenters, truck drivers – all kinds of workers') • In pairs it is used as an alternative to parentheses or brackets (e.g. ' The woman in the red coat – the one with the black bag – was seen in the area shortly afterwards') • Sometimes used to indicate a missing word (e.g. 'the – dog') • In less formal writing the dash is sometimes used as an alternative to the colon to introduce an example, explanation, or amplification (e.g. 'I told you about him before – he was the man who spoke at the conference') • Used to separate units in dates (e.g. 1920–28) or other number spans (e.g. 25–30 per cent)
Apostrophe (')	• Used to show possession (e.g. 'the dog's bone'; 'the children's toys') • Used to show that letters have been missed out of a word in order to contract it, especially in the representation of speech (e.g. 'he is' = 'he's' and 'do not' = 'don't')
Question mark (?)	• Used at the end of the sentence to show that the sentence is a question (e.g. 'What did you say?')
Exclamation mark (!)	• Used to arrest attention and point out something remarkable. Sometimes its use means that the sentence as a whole should be read with emphasis (e.g. 'Maximise your potential!')

The semi-colon (;)

The semi-colon is one of the punctuation marks which is frequently mis-used, so it is worth working through this section carefully if you know that you are not sure about it. If you refer back to the chart you will see that we list two main uses for the semi-colon:

- to indicate the break between equal, co-ordinate clauses in a sentence; it does similar work to the conjunction 'and' (e.g. 'The man in the trench-coat walked towards him; he was carrying a briefcase close to his chest')
- to separate the complex parts of a list.

However, the rules and conventions governing the use of the semi-colon have changed over time, so when you find examples of the semi-colon used in nineteenth-century writing, for instance, you will find that such writers sometimes appear to be misusing it according to conventions of contemporary usage. It is perhaps also true to say that the semi-colon was used much more in nineteenth-century writing than it is today because sentence construction tended to be more complex then. The fact that punctuation conventions have changed through time often poses a significant problem for editors of historical texts: do they adopt a system of punctuation which will make it easier for the twentieth-century reader to read, or do they stay true to the original punctuation? We will show you some examples later in the chapter, but the rules about the use of the semi-colon which we will explain now are rules that apply to *contemporary* writing and publishing conventions.

We have introduced punctuation at this late stage in the book because it is much easier to understand punctuation use when you know something about grammar and grammatical structures in sentences. In an earlier chapter we explained co-ordinate clauses (independent clauses joined together by 'and', 'but' or 'or'). This knowledge is crucial for understanding the rules governing the use of the semi-colon. We can now add that there is a further way of joining together co-ordinate clauses which we did not mention in the earlier chapter and this is by using a semi-colon. This is the main use of the semi-colon.

To illustrate this primary use we'll take a writing scenario. Imagine a press officer called Elaine working in the House of Commons. She is putting the final touches to a press release, editing a number of key sentences in order to make it sound more fluent. Here are two sentences from the document:

The Commons will debate the new Education Bill on Monday. This will lead to an important vote at the end of the week.

Elaine wants to show that there are connections between the two sentences. The full stop here creates too great a separation. What options does she have to indicate a bridge or link between the two sentences?

She could join the two sentences by using a co-ordinating conjunction ('but' and 'or' would be inappropriate here, of course) or she could use a semi-colon:

> The Commons will debate the new Education Bill on Monday   and   this will lead to an important vote at the end of the week.
> The Commons will debate the new Education Bill on Monday   ;   this will lead to an important vote at the end of the week.

These are her choices then:

> The Commons will debate the new Education Bill on Monday *and* this will lead to an important vote at the end of the week.
> The Commons will debate the new Education Bill on Monday; this will lead to an important vote at the end of the week.

Elaine opts to use the semi-colon rather than the conjunction 'and' because she feels that it reads better and is better at indicating the kind of connection she wants to make between the two sentences. Do you agree? She has now joined the two sentences to make one sentence and because of this there is no capital letter after the semi-colon.

It is also possible to make the link between the two independent clauses even more explicit by using both a semi-colon and an adverb such as 'however', 'moreover', 'therefore', 'consequently', 'otherwise', 'nevertheless', 'thus' to indicate how they are connected. Here are some examples:

> I am going to my room; moreover, I intend to stay there for the rest of the day.
> It rained heavily during the afternoon; consequently, we had to cancel the picnic.

In Elaine's case, however, such a conjunction is not really necessary and would probably overload the sentence:

> The Commons will debate the new Education Bill on Monday; *consequently*, this will lead to an important vote at the end of the week.

Sometimes writers use the semi-colon several times in a sentence in order to join together many co-ordinate clauses into one sentence. Here is scientist Charles Darwin, for instance, using the semi-colon in *The Origin of Species*

(1859) to mark out a complex list of pieces of evidence which he wants to set out not as a series of separate sentences but as parts of one long sentence:

> The plants differ considerably in appearance; they have a different flavour and emit a different odour; they flower at slightly different periods; they grow in somewhat different stations; they ascend mountains to different heights; they have different geological ranges; and lastly, according to very numerous experiments made during several years by that most careful observer Gartner, they can be crossed only with much difficulty. We could hardly wish for better evidence of the two forms being specifically distinct.
>
> (Darwin 1986: 105)

Presumably Darwin wanted to arrange them together in one sentence like this because they all prove one thing: that the two forms of the flowers are quite different. Modern writers might choose to use bullet-points to lay out a sentence of this kind.

ACTIVITY 1:

Check through Darwin's long sentence to see whether his use of the semi-colon is correct according to modern conventions of use. Could a full stop be substituted for the semi-colons? Do all the parts contained within the semi-colons form complete independent clauses (including at least a subject and a verb)? Could they stand alone? Read the sentence substituting 'and' for each of the semi-colons. Why did Darwin choose not to use the conjunction 'and' in this sentence (except at the end) do you think?

The prose style of the early twentieth-century novelist Virginia Woolf has often been described as prose-poetry. Her sentences are often long and are carefully crafted to create rhythms and patterns of sound which are very fluid. One of the ways she achieves this is by occasionally using the semi-colon to thread together several shorter sentences or clauses into one longer sentence, just as Charles Darwin did, but for different reasons, in the sentence from *The Origin of Species* we have just looked at. Here, in the 'Time Passes' section of *To the Lighthouse* (1927), she is describing an empty house deteriorating over time. The effect of the whole section 'Time Passes' is much like time-lapse photography:

> Poppies sowed themselves among the dahlias; the lawn waved with long grass; giant artichokes towered among roses; a fringed carnation flowered among the cabbages; while the gentle tapping of a weed at the window had become, on winters' nights, a drumming from sturdy trees and thorned briars which made the whole room green in summer.
>
> (Woolf 1984: 128)

Now look more closely at the last part of Woolf's magnificent sentence ('while the gentle tapping . . . in summer.'). It actually begins with the subordinating conjunction 'while', which tells us that it is a subordinate clause. This means that it is not an independent, free-standing clause. Try writing it out as a sentence and you'll see what we mean. The semi-colon according to contemporary rules and conventions is used to join co-ordinate clauses not a subordinate clause and a main clause, so technically this is a misuse according to contemporary usage. Woolf was writing in 1927 but even if she were writing in 2007 she would be unlikely to follow all the punctuation rules absolutely 'correctly'. Many novelists, poets and dramatists adapt punctuation rules and conventions to suit their own creative purposes. James Joyce, for instance, as we mentioned in Chapter 1, wrote several pieces of prose with no punctuation at all and refused to use inverted commas, which he humorously called 'perverted commas'. However, published writers like Woolf and Joyce are not casual and careless users of punctuation. It is not that they don't care about it; rather, they are likely to be making endless changes to their punctuation until it is exactly right for their purposes. Joyce, for instance, didn't leave out punctuation in the famous Molly Bloom monologue at the end of *Ulysses* because he couldn't be bothered with it, but because he wanted to show the powerful flow and energy of Molly's inner thoughts and didn't want anything to get in the way. So, although punctuation for creative writing is to some extent a matter of personal preference and what we would call 'the rules' are constantly being broken or adapted by such writers, the majority of writing for professional purposes is carefully scrutinised by bosses, publishers, copy-editors and proof-readers for acceptable punctuation. It is important to know how to use the rules correctly and to use the conventions thoughtfully.

An internet site on writing skills run by the University of Birmingham and written by Tom Davies makes an interesting and telling point:

> If you produce work that is mis-spelt and/or badly punctuated and/or ungrammatical, however good the ideas are, people will tend to think that you are stupid. They will be wrong; it will just mean that you can't spell, or can't punctuate, or don't know some of the grammar rules. Nonetheless, that's what they will think. Since it will almost always be in your best interests to show that you are intelligent, rather than stupid, if you have a problem in any of these areas you should do something about it. If you have a word processor, get a spelling checker. Persuade someone you know who can spell, punctuate, etc. to read over your work first and check it: learn the sort of mistakes you make, and don't make them again.

(http://w3.bham.ac.uk/english/bibliography/students/essay)

ACTIVITY 2:

In which of the following sentences has the writer used the semi-colon correctly according to current usage? (Assume for the purposes of this exercise that the punctuation given is the author's, not that of a later editor.) Remember the semi-colon works to join two or more separate and independent clauses so a good test is to substitute a full stop or a co-ordinating conjunction (*and/but/or*) for the semi-colon to see whether all the parts are in fact independent. Every independent clause, remember, should have at least a subject and a verb and be able to form a sentence of its own.

> The window was open; the door too stood open to that best friend of my work, the warm, still sunshine of the wide fields. (Joseph Conrad, letter in Allott 1959: 151)
>
> So I chattered on; and Heathcliff gradually lost his frown, and began to look quite pleasant; when, all at once, our conversation was interrupted by a rumbling sound moving up the road and entering the court. (Emily Brontë 1982: 56)
>
> The package which you sent on Thursday had not arrived; when I left the shop on Saturday morning.
>
> She sits in a chair covered in moth-ravaged burgundy velvet at the low, round table and distributes the cards; sometimes the lark sings, but more often remains a sullen mound of drab feathers. (Angela Carter 1992: 484)

ACTIVITY 3:

Select a non-literary book of any kind (but published in the last twenty years) from your bookshelves and find at least five sentences which use semi-colons. Check to see whether they are correctly used according to current usage and then try to identify why the writer has used them in this particular place. What effect is he or she trying to create? How else might the sentence have been written (i.e. without using a semi-colon)?

Common mistakes in using semi-colons

Sometimes we come across writing in which semi-colons are to be found in almost every sentence and where the writer clearly is using semi-colons in the place of commas or putting them in at almost any point where a break is needed. Such a piece of writing might look like this:

Dear Sir or Madam,

Following your secretary's telephone call; I am enclosing a draft programme for the Induction Course we are proposing to hold from 15 April to 20 April. You will see that following your agreement to speak to the new staff; I have provisionally arranged your session to start at 2.00pm on Wednesday 17 April.

I would like to be able to finalise the arrangements fairly soon; and would therefore be grateful if you could confirm that Wednesday is still convenient for you; and let me have your comments on the programme by Friday of this week; if possible.

ACTIVITY 4:

Correct the punctuation in the letter above.

Semi-colons used in a list

Finally, there is one other use of the semi-colon which you will see on our table. The only other use of the semi-colon is where you are making a series of complex points in a list and a comma does not quite do the job clearly enough. The list must begin with a colon, of course:

Members of the department who share this responsibility are: Rebecca Stott, Head of Department; Peter Cattermole, Field Leader; David Booy, Academic Advisor; and Nigel Wheale, Academic Advisor.

The comma (,)

The comma is the most widely used punctuation mark and there is much variation in its usage. We have shown you how grammatical knowledge is useful for working out how to use a semi-colon correctly. The same is true for some of the uses of the comma. For example, one of its principal uses is to mark out the grammatical structures in a sentence. The table we began with states that there are many uses of the comma but the main ones are:

- to mark out the relationship between independent and dependent clauses (e.g. 'While he waited in the shop, she robbed the safe')
- to show that one phrase or clause in a sentence is being used inside another such as a relative clause (e.g. 'Kevin Jones, who disliked garlic as a boy, found he couldn't live without it') or an introductory phrase

(e.g. 'Reluctantly and with hestitation, Kevin came to admit that he did indeed like garlic')

- to mark a run or list of similar grammatical units (words, phrases, clauses) (e.g. 'the park, the sky, the clouds' or 'He came, he saw, he conquered').

The comma used to mark the relationship between a dependent and independent clause

The first of the above uses is the most complex. We have shown how semi-colons work to join independent clauses (co-ordinate clauses). By contrast, commas mark out the relationship between independent and dependent clauses so if you are not sure about independent and dependent clauses go back to Chapter 1 to revise them. Here are sentences containing a dependent clause and a main, independent clause in which the comma works to mark out the structure:

> As I ran across the room, I slipped on the wet floor.
> If you meet me tomorrow, we can go shopping.
> Because I have lost my glasses, I cannot prepare for the seminar.
> 'As they approached Niagara in the train from Buffalo, Dickens eagerly awaited the sound or sight of the Falls.' (Ackroyd 1990: 365)
> 'While the measurements went on, Darwin wandered about the country.' (Desmond and Moore 1991: 136)

Note that the two clauses in each sentence above are separated by a comma: this is a key use of the comma and in such constructions there is usually no other option. If the dependent clause comes before the independent main clause, the comma is almost always put in. However, if the main clause comes first, the comma can be left out. Be guided here by your sense of what makes for clear reading. Here are the clauses in reverse order so that the main independent clause comes first. Note that the meaning of the sentences is not altered:

> I slipped on the wet floor as I ran across the room.
> We can go shopping if you meet me tomorrow.
> I cannot prepare for the seminar because I have lost my glasses.
> 'Dickens eagerly awaited the sound or sight of the Falls as they approached Niagara in the train from Buffalo.' (Ackroyd 1990: 365 – sentence reversed)
> 'Darwin wandered about the country while the measurements went on.' (Desmond and Moore 1991: 136 – sentence reversed)

The comma used to mark out separate units within sentences

As we said earlier, the primary function of the comma is to mark out the boundaries of units within sentences (words, phrases, clauses) so that they are easier to read. Some people use the comma heavily in their writing and others very sparely. To some extent this is a matter of personal preference. However, there are places in sentences where a comma is necessary in order to mark out a separate unit such as a relative clause or an introductory phrase. We dealt with relative clauses in Chapter 2; turn back to check again if you are not sure you have remembered. A relative clause begins with a relative pronoun ('who', 'whom' (formal), 'whose', 'which', 'that', and 'zero') and 'post-modifies' the noun or noun phrase that precedes it. In the following sentences the relative clause is shown in bold:

> The book *that you bought me* was very useful.
> The tree *that fell during the night* has now been removed.
> The thieves *who took my rings* have been caught.

Relative clauses like this are extremely common in all kinds of writing and in the spoken language too. In each of the cases above, the relative clause is part of the noun phrase – 'The book that you bought me', 'The tree that fell during the night', 'The thieves who took my rings' – and so the relative clause is not separated from the rest of the noun phrase by a comma.

Now consider the difference between the two following sentences:

> The thieves, *who took my rings*, have been caught.
> The thieves *who took my rings* have been caught.

Note that the difference is that in the first sentence the relative clause is marked off from the rest of the sentence by a comma at each end. As a result, the two sentences have different meanings. In the first sentence, 'who took my rings' provides additional information about some thieves – to whom we must assume that the speaker has been previously referring – but this information is incidental and parenthetic to the main point of the sentence. The commas here work in a similar way to brackets. They bracket off an additional piece of information. You could put 'who took my rings' in brackets as a parenthesis and the meaning would be unchanged. In the second sentence you could not put 'who took my rings' in brackets without a change of meaning. 'Who took my rings' is not incidental, parenthetic information, but is part of the noun phrase. 'The thieves' are inseparable from the fact that they took the speaker's rings. If you hyphenated the phrase as 'The thieves-who-took-my-rings' the meaning would not change – though the effect would be fussy and odd. (It has its uses on occasion, though, as in 'The Child-Who-Was-Tired' – the title of a short story by the early twentieth-century writer Katherine Mansfield; it suggests forcibly that the unnamed child has no identity except that of being tired.) The first sentence contains what is called a *non-defining relative clause*, whilst the second sentence contains what is called a *defining relative clause*.

The second kind of separate unit within the sentence that we mentioned is the *introductory phrase or clause*. The following examples include non-finite clauses as well as single words. What is important is that using the comma to mark off the introductory phrase or clause allows the reader to see the beginning of the main clause more clearly:

> Finally, I would like to give my thanks to . . .
> Unaccustomed as I am to public speaking, I would like to address you today . . .
> For one thing, you assume my agreement.
> 'Instead, insects got the upper hand.' (Desmond and Moore 1991: 62)
> 'Overwrought, he plunged headlong into the interior.' (Desmond and Moore 1991: 121)
> 'Stunned at first, Charles broke down as he read.' (Desmond and Moore 1991: 121)

ACTIVITY 5:

Add commas where you think they are needed in the following paragraph from Adrian Desmond and James Moore's biography of Charles Darwin:

> After sailing dangerously in circles for fourteen hours in pitch darkness the Beagle emerged from the Cockburn Channel on 10 June. At long last they had reached the west coast. Setting 'every inch of canvas' she battled out into the long swell of the Pacific the *Adventure* alongside. Here the rugged granite coast pounded by roaring breakers was enough to give landsmen nightmares about 'peril & shipwreck.' Howling northerly gales intensified the effect whipping up angry seas. These were not the only sirens of death. As Fitzroy struggled at the helm the oldest officer lay fighting for his life below-deck.
>
> (Desmond and Moore 1991: 154)

Commas used in lists

In the table the final use of the comma is listed as 'to mark a run or list of similar grammatical units (words, phrases, clauses): e.g. "the park, the sky, the clouds" or "He came, he saw, he conquered" '. The simplest kind of use is in a string of adjectives or nouns such as:

> The menacing, long, low, heavy sigh
> I searched the streets, the lanes, the alleys and the pubs

Punctuation of lists like this is a little more complicated than it seems, however, because there are slight differences of convention between the British punctuation system and the American punctuation system. Look out for these in the books that you read; check to see whether the publisher is American or British. The difference here may seem very small but it is the kind of thing that proof-readers are trained to check for: the American punctuation system uses commas after every item in the list including the last one. The British system does not have a comma after the last item in the list or before the 'and' (if an 'and' is used). The American version of the above sentences would, therefore, look like this:

> The menacing, long, low, heavy, sigh
> I searched the streets, the lanes, the alleys, and the pubs

ACTIVITY 6:

The following sentences need commas and/or semi-colons. Put in the punctuation that you think is needed. In some cases there is more than one option.
  Remember:

- semi-colons act as a kind of co-ordinating conjunction between independent clauses
- you never use commas between independent clauses
- commas are used to show the relationship between independent and dependent clauses in a complex sentence, to indicate a relative clause, for introductory phrases, and in lists.

> Many companies make fat-free ready meals which are very good the food contains a balanced mixture of proteins and vitamins.
> Mr Johnson once ran his own company consequently he is respected and trusted as an entrepreneur.
> The hill was covered with tall stately trees it was a beautiful sight.
> As I turned around I heard a loud thump caused by the dog knocking over the table.
> The house was clean the table set and the food prepared everything was ready for the evening's entertainment.
> The long room which had been used for the dancing was now in a bad state of repair.

The colon (:)

The colon has a precise function distinct from the function of the semi-colon. Like the semi-colon, it separates co-ordinate clauses, but it has a further function, which is to 'stand between' a statement and an explanation or amplification of that statement. It is also used to introduce quotes and lists. Below are some examples:

Standing between a statement and an extension of that statement:
The government has resigned: the vote of confidence was lost.
Shakespeare wrote many of the most famous plays in the world: *Hamlet* and *King Lear* are major examples.
Everyone knows what to do in an emergency: press the fire alarm.
'Thus did the great English novelist meet the great French writer whose work his own most closely resembles: Hugo, the great poet of the poor and the dispossessed, the great chronicler of the urban darkness.' (Ackroyd 1990: 522)

Introducing a list:
The following items were stolen at the time: six rings, a television set, a set of silver cutlery and a CD player.

Introducing a quote:
This idea is suggested in the famous lines of Lord Byron: 'Swung blind and blackening in the moonless air'.

ACTIVITY 7:

Find at least two examples of each of the three different uses of the colon in published books of any kind and write them out. Write a short commentary on why you think they have been used in the sentences you have chosen.

The double dash (– . . . –) and the single dash (–)

A pair of dashes acts like a bracket or parenthesis or like a pair of commas. Below are examples of how these three forms of punctuation are used. All three related forms used to 'bracket off' a unit within a sentence are called *parenthesis*:

> The three forms of parenthesis
> Brackets:
> I told him I couldn't go out to dinner (which was true) and that I'd love to go out with him another time (which was untrue).
>
> Commas:
> His first thought on waking, if he had any thought at all, was to go back to sleep again.
>
> Dashes:
> Please make sure that – if you do want to register with us – you do not forget to fill in the form.

The single dash can substantially alter, or even reverse, the flow of meaning in a statement. For example:

> He is always late – but not today.
> She was delighted to see him – even though she had been very distant on the phone.

The apostrophe (')

The apostophe is a kind of 'raised comma'. It migrated to the English punctuation system from the French punctuation system in the sixteenth century but there was much disagreement about its use until the nineteenth century. There are two main uses of the apostrophe today:

- to show possession (e.g. 'the boy's bike')
- to show where letters are missing from a word or words in order to achieve contraction (e.g. he's = he is, don't = do not).

Possessive apostrophes

It is important that you use these correctly. *This is a rule, not a convention*, particularly in formal, professional writing. However, as possessive apostrophes are perhaps the most widely misused or omitted punctuation mark in informal writing, some people claim that they are on their way to becoming extinct. David Crystal argues that the misuses of the possessive apostrophe are 'understandable, given the long and confused history of this punctuation mark in English' (Crystal 1995: 203).

Possession, or 'belonging to', is normally indicated by adding –'s to the singular noun (i.e. one person or thing) and adding –s' to the plural noun (i.e. more than one person or thing). The following four examples illustrate this:

> Susan's book   the Johnsons' dog
> his master's voice a girls' school

However, for plural nouns which do not end with an 's' (e.g. children, women), add –'s for the possessive form. For example:

> the children's coats   the women's movement

Exceptions sometimes occur when a singular noun already ends with an 's' and thus becomes difficult to pronounce in its possessive form (e.g. Moses's); although conventionally you would add –'s for the singular possessive, it is now becoming more common to add only an apostrophe but no second 's' (e.g. Moses') on such occasions. The general rule then is to be guided by speech; if adding an 's' makes the word difficult to pronounce then you can add only an apostrophe:

> boss's ✔   Charles's ✔   Tess's ✔   Hopkins's ✔   Dickens's ✔
> boss' ✘   Charles' ✘   Tess' ✘   Hopkins' ✔   Dickens' ✔

ACTIVITY 8:

Around the beginning of the twentieth century many banks and large businesses began to drop the apostrophe from their names so that Lloyd's Bank became Lloyds Bank and Barclay's Bank became Barclays Bank. Look around to see how many different kinds of misuse or omission you can find in your local neighbourhood, particularly in shop signs, placards and other notices.

The apostrophe for contraction

In informal writing and in speech we run a number of words together for ease:

> would not = wouldn't
> do not = don't
> he would = he'd
> who is = who's (note not 'whose')
> she will = she'll

In all these cases the apostrophe marks the spot where letters have been taken out. It reminds us what the word is meant to be in its full version.

Its and it's

Many people find it hard to distinguish between the usage of its and it's. The important thing to remember is that:

- you only use the apostrophe when you contract 'it is' to become 'it's'
- you *don't* use the apostrophe for the possessive of 'it'.

In other words:

It's is the abbreviated form of it is.
e.g. It's a sunny day. ✔
Its a sunny day. ✘

Its is a possessive pronoun.
e.g. The cat ate its dinner. ✔
The cat ate it's dinner. ✘

ACTIVITY 9:

Imagine you are a secondary school teacher trying to explain the difference between 'its' and 'it's' to a group of twelve-year-olds. Prepare an A4 work sheet with exercises so that your class will understand the difference. Remember to try to find a way to make the information accessible and memorable for this age group: format, examples and pictures are all very important. The objective here is to design a worksheet that will ensure that these pupils understand and remember the rule permanently!

Rules and conventions

Before we move on to a series of activities which will help you practice your use of punctuation, it is important to remind you about the spectrum of rules and conventions that we mentioned earlier in the chapter. One of the results of the fact that some kinds of punctuation are more optional than others is that some people use a heavy form of comma punctuation and others use a much lighter form of comma punctuation. Both can be correct but the kind of writing you are undertaking will determine your own choices in punctuation use. So long as you stick to the rules we have outlined in this chapter it is up to you whether you put in commas in every pause in a sentence or only put them in where absolutely necessary.

ACTIVITY 10:

Give yourself a few minutes to complete the sentences below, selecting the correct form from the words in brackets.

My friend, (who's/whose) bike I borrowed, wants it back.
(It's/Its) not raining today.
Those books the boys lost were not (there's/theirs/their's).
Our dog has got a thorn in (it's/its) paw.
I say that the money is (your's/yours) but Sue says (it's/its) (her's/hers).
(Theirs/There's/Theres) a wasp on your neck.
We (havent/have'nt/haven't) seen each other for days.
(They've/Theyv'e/Theyve) just gone home.
You (werent/weren't/were'nt) home when I called.
I thought the bike belonged to (James/Jame's/James'), but he said it was (Francis's/Francis) machine.

ACTIVITY 11:

Punctuate the following sentences:

When I lived in Germany for a year I managed to make myself understood even though I speak little German.
Before Pete left Dave lost his temper.
The main towns of Hertfordshire are St Albans Hertford Watford Hatfield and Hemel Hempstead.
Michael Grey my best friend has just broken his leg.
When the rope snapped the climber fell a hundred feet.

ACTIVITY 12:

Write out this paragraph, adding capital letters and punctuation marks where needed.

when i was in london last month i saw david black the young pop star he was jogging down oxford street i rushed up to him and asked him for his autograph unfortunately i had forgotten my pen so he could not sign still it was very exciting to see such a famous person after that we went up the dome of st pauls cathedral and took a trip along the river thames in a glass-topped boat the boat was very crowded so it was quite difficult to see but i was still able to enjoy the trip

---

ACTIVITY 13:

Add punctuation and capitalisation to the following two opening paragraphs from Muriel Spark's short story 'The House of the Poet' (1966) as you think necessary.

In the summer of 1944 when it was nothing for trains from the provinces to be five or six hours late I travelled to London on the night train from Edinburgh which at York was already three hours late there were ten people in the compartment only two of whom I remember well and for good reason

    I have the impression looking back on it of a row of people opposite me dozing untidily with heads askew and as it often seems when we look at sleeping strangers their features had assumed extra emphasis and individuality sometimes disturbing to watch it was as if they had rendered up their daytime talent for obliterating the outward traces of themselves in exchange for mental obliteration in this way they resembled a twelfth-century fresco there was a look of medieval unselfconsciousness about these people all except one.

(Spark 1987: 181)

Summary

In this chapter we have looked at:

- punctuation in co-ordinate clauses, and subordinate clause and main clause constructions
- punctuation in use in varieties of writing
- apostrophes
- contractions in informal writing and speech
- its and it's.

References

Ackroyd, Peter (1990) *Dickens*. London: Sinclair-Stevenson.

Allott, M. (ed.) (1959) *Novelists on the Novel*. London: Routledge.

Brontë, Emily (1982) *Wuthering Heights* [1847], The World's Classics. Oxford: Oxford University Press.

Carter, Angela (1992) 'The Lady of the House of Love' in C. Baldick (ed.), *The Oxford Book of Gothic Tales*. Oxford: Oxford University Press.

Crystal, David (1995) *The Cambridge Encyclopaedia of the English Language*. Cambridge: Cambridge University Press.

Darwin, Charles (1986) *The Origin of Species* [1859]. Harmondswoth: Penguin.

Desmond, A. and Moore, J. (1991) *Darwin*. Harmondsworth: Penguin.

Spark, Muriel (1987) 'The House of the Poet' [1966] in Malcolm Bradbury (ed.), *The Penguin Book of Modern British Short Stories*. Harmondsworth: Penguin.

Woolf, Virginia (1984) *To the Lighthouse* [1927]. London: Granada.

CHAPTER 6

Structures beyond the sentence

Rebecca Stott and Kim Landers

U p to this point in the book we have been concentrating on sentences and units within the sentence to examine grammatical structures and the way these affect and shape varieties of writing. In this chapter we will be taking one step back to look at the bigger picture and to ask: how do sentences fit together to make whole texts? We will consider the structures of texts, placing special emphasis on the paragraph as one of the fundamental building blocks.

Throughout this book we have stressed that language is flexible and that there are a number of different conventions and styles of writing which affect the fundamental structures of the sentence. We have looked at simple and co-ordinate sentences in writing for children and a number of uses for subordinate clauses in more formal writing. So far we have looked at the following varieties of writing:

- writing for children
- short stories
- journalism
- informal letters
- letters
- biography
- guidebooks
- literary writing

in order to stress that when writers make grammatical choices they are influenced by the kind of writing they are producing and the audiences they are writing for.

This is true, too, for structures beyond the sentence; the way people organise their sentences on the page depends on what they want to say and who they are saying it to. This is not confined to professional writers; we all do it all the time, adapting the order of what we say or write for particular purposes. Instinctively, we find ways of structuring our message to make it comprehensible and effective. Storytellers, for instance, try to create suspense with their opening sentences, to keep their audiences' attention as the story develops. Tabloid journalists use very short paragraphs to maintain their readers' interest. As readers, we expect and tolerate different things from the different texts that we read. We might find a novel that plays around with time and sequence stimulating and challenging, but if the writer of a set of instructions for programming a video played around with sequence and word order it would be very irritating indeed.

Genre and text structure

Many forms of writing have an instant format or structure, one that almost never varies. Think about recipes, for instance. We all know exactly how a recipe is going to be laid out on a page. We also expect the cooking instructions to be written in compressed sentences in a clear sequence so that we can follow each of the instructions in the right order, whilst we are cutting and chopping and stirring.

Tomato sauce with olives and oregano
Serves 4 people

800g ripe tomatoes (the riper the better)
100g black olives
1 tablespoon of roughly chopped fresh oregano (or 1–2 tsp dried oregano)
2 tablespoons olive oil
3 cloves crushed garlic
350g spaghetti

1. Put the tomatoes in a basin and cover with boiling water for up to a minute. Drain the water and once cool skin the tomatoes. Roughly chop and remove the seeds and any tough stalks.
2. Put the olive oil and garlic in a saucepan, turn on heat to medium, and gently cook for 1 minute. Add the chopped and stoned black olives. Stir for one minute then add the chopped tomatoes and about 2/3 of the chopped oregano. Simmer on a gentle heat until the tomatoes have broken down and the sauce has thickened (about 20 minutes).
3. Meanwhile, cook the spaghetti as directed on the packet. Add a drop of olive oil to the cooked, drained spaghetti to prevent it sticking and place it in a serving dish. When the tomato sauce is ready, season and add the

rest of the oregano and cook for a further minute. Pour the sauce onto the spaghetti and serve.

(Recipe donated by Tory Young)

The structure of this recipe is divided into two sections: a list of ingredients and a set of instructions for cooking. However, we can also see that the instructions for cooking are laid out as a kind of list, using compressed sentences, and that these instructions are divided into three separate larger units. In the writer's mind there are three main stages in preparing the dish and many more minor stages within the three larger sections. She has arranged her ideas and instructions into small units and larger units.

If this same writer were writing in a different format – say she had been asked to produce a review of a cookery book for publication – she would not use numbered items as here in her recipe, but paragraphs to indicate the main units of her text. Here is a review of a cookery book taken from the internet:

Recipes from the French wine harvest

Vintage feasts from the vineyards

by Rosi Hanson

Published by Cassell at Stg 18.99

with photographs by Katerina Kalogeraki

ISBN 0-304-34540-7

This book is quite the most brilliant idea, combining marvellous descriptions of the classic wine growing regions of France at harvest time, with mouth watering recipes from the immense variety of traditional farmhouse fare that sustains the workers toiling in both vineyard and *cave*.

Napoleon observed that an army marches on its stomach. This is certainly true of the motley army of pickers, including students, factory workers, wine-buffs, gypsies and ski-bums as well as the extended family of the vineyard proprietors, who are all united by a common love of good wine and food.

The preparations begin months before the harvest: fruit and vegetables are bottled in advance, with jams and preserves to enliven the breakfasts. Terrines and patés for the picnic lunches in the vines are prepared a few days in advance with *estouffades* and *pot au feu* to warm up cold bones after a chilly autumn day out of doors on a damp hillside.

Each region, from the Loire and Champagne to Alsace in the North, from the classic regions of Bordeaux and Burgundy, to the Rhone Valley in the South, has its distinctive style based on local ingredients, its terroir and its traditions. Sadly, some of the proprietors no longer do the catering themselves, except perhaps at the end of the vintage when there is a grand party before the army is demobbed to the four corners of the globe. In Burgundy this feast is known as *la Paulée*, and *La Paulée de Meursault* is one of *Les Trois Glorieuses*, the grand series of events that mark the climax of the auction at the *Hospice de Beaune*.

Because of the author's long association with Burgundy, it is this region that takes pride of place, though all the others get a very fair crack of her whisk! After an introduction to the harvest in each region, Rosi Hanson gives entertaining accounts of some of the fascinating characters and the feasts peculiar to the district or even property. She managed to get into the kitchens of some of the great names of the French wine world, but it is her descriptions of essentially simple local fare that are amongst the most satisfying.

The photographs are beautifully evocative of both place and platter. I particularly loved the picture of the fabulously restored *vendagers'* dining room at Chateau Loudenne, and I would never have believed that a humble poached egg in red wine sauce could look so delicious. Who says the French don't enjoy a cooked breakfast?

This book would make a super Christmas present for someone who likes wine and enjoys messing about in the kitchen. None of the recipes are all that complicated, but they really do conjure up a rather old fashioned France, far removed from trendy styles or *nouvelle cuisine*.

(Clifford Mould on http://www.winedine.co.uk)

ACTIVITY 1:

This review has been divided into seven paragraphs. What is distinctive about each paragraph? Does the review begin with the particular and move to the general or vice versa? How have the ideas been arranged? How successful is the structure of the review in conveying the ideas of the reviewer? How else might it have been ordered?

What is a paragraph?

Literally, it means a unit of written language which comes between the sentence and the full text. It is marked out by an indentation at the beginning of the paragraph or by a blank line between one paragraph and the next. Just as punctuation visually indicates the structure of the sentence, paragraph indentations mark out the 'building blocks' of the larger piece of prose writing.

A paragraph groups together a number of sentences which are all linked in some way. Each paragraph has one main idea or proposition or part of a story to tell. So the movement from one paragraph to another is crucial because we rely on the writer to give us clear signals of changes of subject, focus or direction. The visual signal of the gap between the paragraphs prepares us for the change. As we embark on the new unit, a good writer will tell us quite quickly, often in what's called the *topic sentence*, what the new set of ideas will be, and how the text as a whole – the argument or the plot – is developing. Writers give their audiences an idea of the underlying structure of the text through language and linking devices (*cohesion*) and through a logical flow of ideas (*coherence*). Cohesion and coherence are both achieved in part through paragraph structuring.

What is coherence?

Coherence is the first essential in a text, a recognisable structure of thought and ideas. It is created partly by the writer or speaker, but also partly by the reader or listener, who responds to the signals given by the text. Because of this double nature, coherence is a complex matter to analyse, though it is not difficult to produce. It depends on a context of culture, attitudes and knowledge which aren't always consciously recognised or shared by the producer of the text or by its audience.

Coherence and prediction

We 'know' certain things about the world, the universe and everything: that the world is at the centre of the universe or that it is the third planet orbiting round a minor sun in an unimportant galaxy; that there's a Queen of England; that swallows hibernate or that they fly south for the winter. We speak, listen, write and read in the context of this 'knowledge'. Similarly, the cultures we live in inform our attitudes, influencing not only our social and political choices, but also the way we express ourselves. In our use of language, prediction of what is coming next operates at all levels, from being able to complete someone else's sentence for them to being pretty sure that a story beginning 'Once upon a time . . .' will end with '. . . and they all lived happily ever after' or something very like it. Prediction plays a large part in our communications, and it is made possible, not just by shared language, but by shared knowledge and culture.

Coherence makes use of this by creating expectations which are then met. There are exceptions: humour often works by upsetting expectations, for example in the following joke from Douglas Adams's *Hitchhiker's Guide to the Galaxy* (1979):

'It's unpleasantly like being drunk.'
'What's so unpleasant about being drunk?'
'You ask a glass of water.'

(Adams 1979: 47)

But the exceptions demonstrate just how pervasive our assumptions are, in literary as well as non-literary discourse.

Look at this extract from the novel *Villette* by Charlotte Brontë, published in 1853. Brontë's novel tells the story of the early life of a young woman, Lucy Snowe, about how she goes to Brussels and starts to teach in a school and eventually falls in love with a teacher there called Paul Emmanuel. Most novel readers of the 1850s would probably have expected the story to have ended with a clear resolution of the plot, almost certainly a marriage, the formulaic closure to this kind of novel. Brontë was clearly aware of these expectations, but perhaps she was irritated by them; certainly she took a risk with the ending of *Villette*, though she could not break with the convention entirely. In the final paragraphs she tells us that Paul Emmanuel is in a shipwreck.

Here pause: pause at once. There is enough said. Trouble no quiet, kind heart; leave sunny imaginations hope. Let it be theirs to conceive the delight of joy born again fresh out of great terror, the rapture of rescue from peril, the wondrous reprieve from dread, the fruition of return. Let them picture union and a happy succeeding life.

(Brontë 1985: 596)

In other words she does not tell us what happens next. She says effectively 'if you like books that end with happy marriages, then imagine this one ending that way. I'm not going to tell you either way. It's up to you to decide what happens to these people.' She takes the formulaic plot structure of her time (young girl ⇒ adventures ⇒ marriage) and breaks the final component (marriage) in order to show people that this sequence that they expect in books is preconditioned; there may be all sorts of other things that happen to women apart from marriage, which could make the final part of the sequence that we call a novel. For all text-types, coherence depends on the organisation and satisfaction of readers' predictions, or, of course, their frustration if you want a shock effect to make them think, as Brontë does.

The kind of coherence a reader expects from a piece of writing depends to some extent upon context. Generally readers are much more tolerant of lower levels of coherence in poetry than in other kinds of texts, particularly when the poet is well known. Readers of poetry usually expect to have to puzzle out meanings; it is part of the experience of reading poetry. The same would also be true of philosophical or theological books. However, if the same readers were to pick up a guidebook or an instruction manual they would expect much higher levels of immediate coherence. Thus different situations, text-types and genres offer different contexts, sending different signals which trigger different predictions from their audiences.

ACTIVITY 2:

Choose a novel you have read recently or a film you have seen which has an ending which you have found disappointingly predictable. Identify the sequence of events in the novel or film in broad 'blocks' of action. Define in what way the final 'block' of the plot might be regarded as satisfying the readers' or audiences' expectations in a rather predictable way. Then rewrite the final section of the plot in order to challenge those expectations.

Organising coherence

Ways of organising coherence vary according to text-type as discussed earlier. In presenting an argument, for example, coherence can come from a logically ordered sequence of ideas, the classic structure of introduction, development and conclusion. In fiction, it can be created by a strong narrative voice, or by the time sequence: in Jane Austen's *Persuasion*, for example, the passage of time is strongly marked with such phrases as 'thirteen years ago', 'these two months', 'eight years, almost eight years, had passed', 'a few days had made a change indeed', 'could she have believed it a week ago'.

Look at this example from the opening paragraphs of Terry Pratchett's novel *Small Gods* (1992):

> Now consider the tortoise and the eagle.
> The tortoise is a ground-living creature. It is impossible to live nearer the ground without being under it. Its horizons are a few inches away. It has about as good a turn of speed as you need to hunt down a lettuce. It has survived while the rest of evolution flowed past it by being, on the whole, no threat to anyone and too much trouble to eat.
> And then there is the eagle. A creature of the air and high places, whose horizons go all the way to the edge of the world. Eyesight keen enough to spot the rustle of some small and squeaky creature half a mile away. All power, all control. Lightning death on wings. Talons and claws enough to make a meal of anything smaller than it is and at least take a hurried snack out of anything bigger.

And yet the eagle will sit for hours on the crag and survey the king-doms of the world until it spots a distant movement and then it will focus, focus, *focus* on the small shell wobbling among the bushes down there on the desert. And it will *leap* . . .

And a minute later the tortoise finds the world dropping away from it. And it sees the world for the first time, no longer one inch from the ground but five hundred feet above it, and it thinks: what a great friend I have in the eagle.

And then the eagle lets go.

And almost always the tortoise plunges to its death. Everyone knows why the tortoise does this. Gravity is a habit that is hard to shake off. No one knows why the eagle does this . . .

(Pratchett 1992: 1)

These two characters, the eagle and the tortoise, disappear for most of the rest of the novel, but they return at a moment of climax, when a tortoise, dropping from the sky, saves the hero from being sacrificed by a fanatical high priest, because it drops on the priest's head and kills him. It is a spectacular moment in the book, all the more successful because of the return of the first characters in the book, if only for a few dramatic moments.

But let us look at the extract itself. It is a unit in itself, almost a short story, similar to one of Aesop's Fables. It is a story within a story and Pratchett, aware of its fable-like quality, uses the structuring conventions of fable to create coherence. It is strongly sequential with the following structure of main points:

Tortoise = close to ground, no threat to anyone, inedible
Eagle = high up, powerful, can catch anything it wants to eat
and yet sometimes an eagle leaps and catches a tortoise
and sometimes a tortoise gets carried off and sees the world from above
and sometimes an eagle drops a tortoise
and then the tortoise plunges to its death because gravity is a hard habit to break

The story is a chain of events which Pratchett offers us as an inevitable, ages-old, seen-by-all observation of the natural world. The repeated 'and's make the sequence sound even more pre-programmed and inevitable: 'and then . . . and sometimes . . . and yet . . . and a minute later'. But what he is describing is in fact bizarre and fantastic. After all, how many tortoises have you seen dropping from the sky recently? Pratchett makes consider-able significance of his carefully constructed series of paragraphs in which he underlines the differences between the two creatures and the way they see the world. Finally, 'gravity is a hard habit to break' indicates an element of satire because what is really inevitable in this story is not that eagles will keep on dropping tortoises but rather that a heavy object will always fall to the ground when dropped from a great height. It is that object dropped from a great height that will play a major and quite unexpected role in the climax of the story at a much later point.

What is cohesion and how does it work?

Cohesion is an idea which is mostly used to look at how sub-units within a text (sentences, question and answer, paragraphs, verses, chapters) hold together. It refers to the way a speaker or writer uses the built-in relationships between words, phrases and sentences to create a sense of shape and 'connectedness'. Usually, we employ a wide range of cohesive devices in writing, more or less consciously, and we will explore the main categories here.

Cohesion in choice of words

In ordinary language use we create a basic cohesion primarily by choosing related words and phrases. In any individual text, the vocabulary will probably be consistent in terms of register and the vocabulary with which the writer assumes the audience is familiar. So a book of critical essays will use a formal vocabulary and specialised literary terms, while a conversation in the pub will be slangy and informal, avoiding specialised expressions, and anyone breaking these conventions is likely to be mocked and in extreme cases rapidly left to drink alone.

This patterning can be broken, of course, for particular effect: when Shaw, in his play *Pygmalion*, made his Cockney heroine say 'not bloody likely' at an ultra-respectable tea party, he was making a point about class and the English language; when D.H. Lawrence used four-letter words in *Lady Chatterley's Lover*, he was making a point about English attitudes to sex. Both writers were breaking the conventions for shock effect.

Cohesion of language is at least partly a matter of style. James Kelman's way of writing, for example, is very distinctive. In this opening to his short story 'By the Burn', while he's breaking some rules ('don't use bad language'), he's also setting up a particular style of spoken language:

> Fucking bogging mud man a swamp, an actual swamp, it was fucking a joke. He pulled his foot clear but the boot was still lodged there like it was quicksand and it was going to get sucked off and vanish down into it forever. He felt the suction hard on his foot but when he pulled, curling his toes as firm as possible, out it came with a loud squelching sound. Thank Christ for that. He shook his head, studying the immediate area, these

marshy stalks of grass were everywhere; fucking hopeless. He glanced back across the wide expanse of waste ground and up to where the blocks of flats were. But he had to go this way and go this way right now, he was late enough as it was, he just couldn't afford to waste any time.

(Kelman 1991: 239)

Here the informal, colloquial register is that of spoken English, more particularly, of course, spoken Scots, and this, sustained throughout the story, along with a vocabulary of specific and physical detail, holds the narrative very firmly together.

Patterns of repetition and reiteration

Repetition is conventionally seen as a sign of bad style, but in fact we use it quite a lot as a cohesive device. Inevitably key words are reused throughout a text like a chorus, as we have seen in the Terry Pratchett example, for instance. Just as writers can repeat words throughout a text to create a pattern and a structure, they might also use repeated sentence constructions to create unity of structure and this is called 'parallelism' or sometimes 'syntactic parallelism'. There are many versions of parallelism, which simply means patterns of syntax either within a sentence or across several sentences. It might be formed by using:

- an identical syntactic structure in each clause
- an identical or similar length to each clause
- a similar rhythm in each clause
- an antithetical balance within or between clauses.

It is used a great deal in persuasive writing and speaking, particularly in formal speeches, because it can add emphasis, clarity, a sense of balance, cumulative weight or the sense of building to a climax.

ACTIVITY 3:

Here are a number of examples of different kinds of parallelism from President Clinton's inaugural address of 1993. Identify the repeated structures or combinations of words used in each case and identify what you think the use of parallelism has added to the sentence or paragraph:

Today we celebrate the mystery of American renewal.
    This ceremony is held in the depth of winter. But, by the words we speak and the faces we show the world, we force the spring.

A spring reborn in the world's oldest democracy, that brings forth the vision and courage to reinvent America.

[...]

Each generation of Americans must define what it means to be an American.

[...]

Today, a generation raised in the shadows of the Cold War assumes new responsibilities in a world warmed by the sunshine of freedom but threatened still by ancient hatreds and new plagues.

Raised in unrivaled prosperity, we inherit an economy that is still the world's strongest, but is weakened by business failures, stagnant wages, increasing inequality, and deep divisions among our people.

[...]

Communications and commerce are global; investment is mobile; technology is almost magical; and ambition for a better life is now universal. We earn our livelihood in peaceful competition with people all across the earth.

Profound and powerful forces are shaking and remaking our world, and the urgent question of our time is whether we can make change our friend and not our enemy.

This new world has already enriched the lives of millions of Americans who are able to compete and win in it. But when most people are working harder for less; when others cannot work at all; when the cost of health care devastates families and threatens to bankrupt many of our enterprises, great and small; when fear of crime robs law-abiding citizens of their freedom; and when millions of poor children cannot even imagine the lives we are calling them to lead – we have not made change our friend.

[...]

Our democracy must be not only the envy of the world but the engine of our own renewal. There is nothing wrong with America that cannot be cured by what is right with America.

[...]

It will not be easy; it will require sacrifice. But it can be done, and done fairly, not choosing sacrifice for its own sake, but for our own sake. We must provide for our nation the way a family provides for its children.

[...]

We must do what America does best: offer more opportunity to all and demand responsibility from all.

(http://www.indiana.edu/~libgpd/guides/pres/pres42.htm)

Connective words and phrases

A number of words and phrases (usually conjunctions and adverbs) act as markers of various types of links. Within a sentence, the obvious example is 'and', but there are others which signal connections in the text as a whole. The main categories are:

Connective words	Examples
Addition	and, in addition, furthermore
Contrast	but, however, on the other hand
Alternative	or, alternatively, another possibility
Time	then, later, finally
Example	for instance, in particular
Cause	so, as a result, therefore

These explicit connections are often implicit in conversation (e.g. 'It was raining stair-rods this afternoon. I got soaked through. Had to go home and dry out') where cause and effect are there but do not need to be marked. In any complex, formal discussion in speech or writing, such as an academic essay, these links are vital to clarify the structure of the argument. Here's an example, where we have used italic to show the connectives. Imagine Sherlock Holmes and Dr Watson discussing their latest case.

'*Firstly*, Watson,' said Holmes, meditatively playing an arpeggio on his violin, 'I think we should consider who had the opportunity to perpetrate this appalling crime.'

'Well, Holmes, the victim's husband, Lord Alfred, left his club early and didn't return home until midnight. Said he couldn't find a cab.'

'He has no alibi, *therefore*. *Then* there is Miss Armitage-Twistleton, the companion, who says she attended a concert of chamber music.'

'*However*, no-one saw her there. *Next* we must consider the butler. He had the evening off and went to a public house, *but* the landlord does not remember serving him after 9 o'clock.'

'*Consequently*, he also is without an alibi. Who else is there?'

'*In addition*, we have the housekeeper, who was alone in her room all evening. The maids, *on the other hand*, were together until bedtime.'

'So they at least are out of it. *To sum up*, then, we have four possible murderers. *Now* for the motive. Of these four, who would have a reason for smothering Lady Ermyntrude with her own bustle?'

'At least three of them, I'm afraid, Holmes.' A ruddy tinge suffused Watson's honest features. 'I'm sorry to have to tell you that Lord Alfred and Miss Armitage-Twistleton were conducting an extra-marital intrigue.'

'Good heavens! They must both, *as a result*, be suspected of wishing his wife out of the way.'

'*In addition*, the butler was carrying on an amatory relationship with the housekeeper, and resented Lady Ermyntrude's strongly expressed disapproval.'

'*Then* he also is a suspect. And the housekeeper?'

'Ah, now she, *in contrast*, appeared devoted to Lady Ermyntrude.'

'*But* have we proof of that?' Holmes returned sharply.

'I fear not.'

'*Finally*, then, we have four people with opportunity and possible motives. This is going to be a delightfully tricky case, Watson.'

(Kim Landers – with apologies to Arthur Conan Doyle)

ACTIVITY 4:

Re-read this passage. Do you find other types of cohesion, apart from the connectives and adverbs, such as repetition, parallel structures and paraphrase, for instance? Imagine you are a scriptwriter for a television drama. Write out a short script for the two lead women police detectives discussing a case, and speculating upon the identity of the murderer, using as many of the connectives identified in italic, in the passage above, as you can.

ACTIVITY 5:

Below is a list of sentences taken from one paragraph in a book about writing by Vivian Summers called *Clear English* (1991). We have jumbled up the sentence order. Reassemble the sentence order of the paragraph using only the clues provided in the five sentences themselves. What clues are you looking for in reassembling the sentence order? The author is summarising points for and against a particular view on how English should be studied.

> It also makes the study of English difficult, laborious and, for the majority of pupils, just plain boring.
> This sees English as a system obeying rules of grammar and sentence structure which have to be learned in detail and applied rigorously.
> It does not even automatically produce good writing, hence the swing to the freer and less structured approach of the post-war period with its emphasis on 'creative writing' rather than the rules of grammar.
> An opposing point of view is widely regarded as the old-fashioned one.
> It seems academically respectable because it makes the study of English similar to that of Latin – for centuries the staple of English education. (Summers 1991: 10)

When you have reassembled the paragraph, identify the clues that made it possible for you to rediscover the original sequence of the sentences. What have you learned from this exercise about the ordering of sentences and creating links between one sentence and another? Write up your answers in the form of a short commentary.

ACTIVITY 6:

We have taken three paragraphs from a chapter in *Clear English* (including the one above so this is an opportunity to check your reassembled paragraph) and jumbled them up. We have numbered them to help you in your re-ordering. Decide on the running order of the three paragraphs. What clues are you looking for in making these decisions and how coherent and cohesive is it as a piece of writing? What devices does it use for creating coherence and cohesion between paragraphs? Write out a summary of these devices.

1. Although the new method had its successes, it was not the complete answer. Students undoubtedly produced more interesting and imaginative pieces of work under the old system, but they lacked a firm knowledge of the way language works and the security this brings in writing grammatically. Readers are very quick to detect errors in punctuation and lapses in grammar, yet too many students brought up on 'creative' writing are unable to explain when it is correct to use a comma, a semi-colon or even a full stop and what makes a sentence a sentence!

2. An opposing point of view is widely regarded as the old-fashioned one. This sees English as a system obeying rules of grammar and sentence structure which have to be learned in detail and applied rigorously. It seems academically respectable because it makes the study of English similar to that of Latin – for centuries the staple of English education. It also makes the study of English difficult, laborious and, for the majority of pupils, just plain boring. It does not even automatically produce good writing, hence the swing to the freer and less structured approach of the post-war period with its emphasis on 'creative writing' rather than the rules of grammar.

3. There are two schools of thought about learning to write. One says that the skills will be best learned by experiencing 'language in practice' in all its varieties, written and spoken. It believes that mastery of expression is caught rather than taught and that a student who is motivated to write will find the way to do so. The role of the teacher is to provide this varied language experience through books and recordings and by devising situations that will stimulate the student to explore language for himself. The teacher then provides advice and guidance as required. This attitude has been in the forefront of the teaching of English for the last twenty years or more.

(Summers 1991: 10–11)

Topic sentences

You will notice in Vivian Summers's clearly ordered paragraphs that each one begins with a statement of the key point of the paragraph. This is called a 'topic sentence'. Each of her paragraphs begins with a topic sentence and the rest of the paragraph expands on, or explores further, or provides evidence for that initial point. Topic sentences are particularly useful in writing that seeks to make a case, because the reader can clearly see the series of points that are being put together to form the whole argument. In fact where writers are particularly strong on topic sentences it is sometimes possible to gather the main lines of the argument simply from reading the first sentence of each paragraph of the chapter or essay. Of course, the topic sentence is usually but not always the first sentence in the paragraph. Some writers keep their topic sentences to the last sentence. This creates a very different effect because you move through evidence and detail to the main point rather than beginning with it.

Occasionally topic sentences are to be found somewhere in the middle of the paragraph. Some computer software programmes have programmes which will take a document and summarise it. All such programmes do is to take the first sentence of each paragraph and delete everything else. Thus such programmes are beginning with a major assumption – that every paragraph of the document will begin with a topic sentence. This is not always the case.

ACTIVITY 7:

Choose a chapter in a book or an essay by an academic writer. Read it carefully through once and then attempt to identify the topic sentence in each paragraph. Remember not to assume that it will always be the first sentence. Put together all the topic sentences and assess how complete a sense this gives you of the whole argument.

You will by now have realised that when paragraphs in expository prose particularly are not entirely successful it is usually because they lack, within themselves, one or more of the following: an orderly sequence, a logical progression from point to point, a balance between the claims made and the evidence offered, and a lack of integration with what comes before or after. They often also lack lucid statements of the points to be made in each paragraph (topic sentences). Clarity of expression, of course, goes hand-in-hand with clarity of mind and organisation. If you know what you want to say, you can say it clearly (though sometimes after several attempts).

ACTIVITY 8:

Find four examples of introductory paragraphs to academic essays or books. Analyse them for coherence and for the way in which the sentences follow on from each other in a coherent way. Choose the introduction which you think is weakest and rewrite it in order to increase the clarity and coherence.

ACTIVITY 9:

Choose an essay you have written recently which you feel would benefit from further editing. If you are working in groups exchange essays so that everyone is working on someone else's essay. If you are working alone, in order to achieve a maximum amount of objectivity, you might want to think of it as another student's essay. Your task is to come up with a series of helpful and constructive suggestions for improving the shape and paragraph structure of the essay. As you do this you might want to consider the following questions:

- Are the ideas clear?
- What's the structure of the argument? Is the structure made clear to the reader?
- Is it helped or hindered by the paragraphing?
- Does the opening signal what's coming?
- Does the ending wrap it up adequately?
- Does the writer use cohesive signals to help the reader, e.g. connectives and adverbs?
- Does the writer use topic sentences to signal the key points of the paragraphs?

When you have made notes on these questions, write a short commentary for the student (as if you were a tutor) suggesting ways in which s/he might rewrite it and/or restructure it to make it more coherent and effective.

ACTIVITY 10:

You are about to write a formal letter of complaint to a firm of plumbers who have recently completed some work on your house. You want to include the following points and complaints:

- that they have not made good the damage they caused to the bathroom floor
- that they charged for work they did not do
- the reason why you are writing
- that they left an electrical socket underneath the bath
- that you had heard good reports about their work
- that the pipes were not welded together properly and have been leaking
- that you have had to call in another firm of plumbers to repair the work they did
- that they have not been answering the phone
- that you will write to the Council to report them
- that they did not give you a formal invoice for the work
- that they took twice as long to complete the work than they said they would
- that you want them to refund some of the money you paid
- that you will write to the local newspapers to ask them to withdraw their advert.

Put these random points into some kind of order for a letter of complaint that will be constructed in two to four paragraphs (you decide on how many). Then write out a plan which will indicate the main function of each paragraph with all the individual points listed under the paragraph headings. Then write out the letter using connective words where possible to create a letter of complaint that is polite, firm, concise and has clear objectives.

Summary

In this chapter we have looked at:

- the function of paragraphs
- different structuring patterns of varieties of writing
- sequencing ideas
- coherence
- cohesion
- using connectives.

References

Adams, Douglas (1979) *Hitchhiker's Guide to the Galaxy*. London: Pan.
Brontë, Charlotte (1985) *Villette* [1853]. Harmondsworth: Penguin.
Kelman, James (1991) 'By the Burn' in *The Burn*. London: Secker and Warburg.
Pratchett, Terry (1992) *Small Gods*. London: Corgi.
Summers, Vivian (1991) *Clear English*. Harmondsworth: Penguin.

Grammar and style

Val Scullion

Throughout this book we have been exploring grammar both as a way of reflecting on and improving your own writing techniques and as a way of understanding the grammatical choices that established writers make in order to achieve particular effects. Grammar and sentence structure are the concerns of all writers. Joseph Conrad famously described the struggle, commitment and pleasure of writing prose fiction as:

> an unremitting never-discouraged care for the shape and ring of sentences
> . . . My task which I am trying to achieve is, by the power of the written
> word to make you hear, to make you feel – it is before all, to make you
> see.

> (Conrad 1977: 12)

We argued in Chapter 1 that a closer knowledge of grammatical structures helps us to appreciate and analyse the skills of other writers. Virginia Woolf uses physical metaphors in *A Room of One's Own* (1929) when she describes picking up a novel in order to find out whether the novelist 'has a pen in her hand or a pickaxe'. She tries 'a sentence or two on [her] tongue'. Hearing, feeling, 'tasting' and seeing the patterns and structures of language reveals the infinitely variable and subtle stylistic effects that individual writers create. To savour the sentence, then, is to understand style. In this chapter we will focus on prose style and analyse several texts by using a predominantly grammatical approach.

Passage 1: *Great Expectations* by Charles Dickens

Here is a famous passage from Dickens's *Great Expectations* (1861). It describes a room in the house of Miss Haversham, an aged, embittered woman who, many years before, had been jilted on her wedding day. It is presented from the point of view of the novel's narrator, Pip, who is remembering his experiences as a young boy. Newly introduced into the room, he looks around, scanning the space, focusing on one object after another. The visual effect of the prose is rather like a panning camera. Although the room contains many familiar objects, such as a fireplace, clock, table and tablecloth, it is nevertheless strange. We share Pip's angle of vision, but more importantly, his unease and his perception of the damp, decaying atmosphere of the place. As he observes the inanimate objects, they seem to become surreal and outside the 'normal' ordering of things. How is this effect created? In particular, which grammatical features of style create a suggestion of menace? The nouns have been identified in italic to aid your stylistic analysis.

> I [Pip] crossed the staircase *landing*, and entered the *room* she indicated. From that *room*, too, the *daylight* was completely excluded, and it had an airless *smell* that was oppressive. A *fire* had been lately kindled in the damp, old-fashioned *grate*, and it was more disposed to go out than to burn up, and the reluctant *smoke* which hung in the *room* seemed colder than the clearer *air* – like our own marsh *mist*. Certain wintry *branches* of *candles* on the high *chimney-piece* faintly lighted the *chamber*: or, it would be more expressive to say, faintly troubled its *darkness*. It was spacious, and I dare say had once been handsome, but every discernible *thing* in it was covered with *dust* and *mould*, and dropping to *pieces*. The most prominent *object* was a long *table* with a *tablecloth* spread on it, as if a *feast* had been in *preparation* when the *house* and the *clock* all stopped together. An *epergne* or *centre-piece* of some *kind* was in the *middle* of this *cloth*; it was so heavily overhung with *cobwebs* that its *form* was quite indistinguishable; and, as I looked along the yellow *expanse* out of which it seemed to grow, like a black *fungus*, I saw speckled-legged *spiders* with blotchy *bodies* running *home* to it, and running out from it, as if some *circumstance* of the greatest public *importance* had just transpired in the spider *community*.
>
> (Dickens 1953: 81–2)

Dickens's style in this passage is noun-centred (or 'nominal', which is the adjective from noun). The high proportion of words functioning as nouns shows this to be so. Most of them are concrete nouns and could serve as an inventory of the room. Their effect is to make the setting particularised in the closest detail – a gift for any film-maker and a feast for the imagination! In addition, the nouns (forty-two in all) are heavily qualified by adjectives.

A high proportion of adjectives (which can occupy both a pre- and post-modifying position in relation to the nouns) stand in a pre-modifying position and therefore, by means of this syntactical structure, reduce wordiness. This grammatical choice makes the prose dense and textured, giving the impression of suffocation and clutter. Thus grammar and meaning reinforce each other.

Description of objects in the room shows them to be both domestic and strange. For example, a clock, even a stopped clock, is a familiar domestic item. But in this room it has metaphoric resonance beyond its immediate setting. This is implied by the grammatical structure of the sentence in which it is collocated with the noun 'house' as co-ordinated subject of the verb 'stopped'. Houses do not literally stop. Consequently, both house *and* clock are likely to be metaphoric, representing concepts such as family, family history and the passage of time.

The nominal style of the text in question also creates an impression of Pip standing motionless. It implies that he was static for some time and subject to the effect of his surroundings, rather than capable of affecting them. Nominalisation is reinforced by personification as objects in the room take on a life of their own. For example, the fire was 'disposed' to go out, the candles 'troubled' the darkness and mould grew insidiously. These effects combine to suggest Pip's vulnerability. The minute description slows down the pace of the narrative to something approaching our common experience of time. This feature of Dickens's text accords with Ian Watt's description of the realist novel (Watt 1957: 27). He argues that the realist mode of writing is characterised by an exhaustive presentation of a recognisable 'reality', a presentation that is so detailed and specific that we might mistake it for a transcription, rather than a imaginative version of the phenomenal world (35). The realist novelist, Watt maintains, places characters 'in a background of particularised time and place', vividly realising a moment in their lives (26). This aptly describes the style and subject matter of the Dickens passage.

ACTIVITY 1:

This activity encourages you to consider the stylistic effect of adjectives, and nouns used as adjectives, when they are placed in pre-modifying (before the noun) and post-modifying (after the noun) positions in a sentence (by using the verb 'to be'). The novelist Fay Weldon has an unequivocal opinion on this matter, at least in the book called *Letters to Alice* (1984) in which she takes the role of a fictional aunt writing a series of letters to her niece Alice, who wants to write a novel:

> I don't like too many adjectives or adverbs – I say if a noun or a verb is worth describing, do it properly, take a sentence to do it. There's no hurry.

(Weldon 1984: 99–100)

Dickens's text obviously bears no resemblance to Weldon's distinctively expansive style. Rewrite two or three sentences of the passage from *Great Expectations*, putting into practice Weldon's advice by expanding the number of sentences to find other ways of describing the room which avoid using adjectives and adverbs. Compare the style of the original text with your own rewritten version. What is lost and gained in this change of style?

ACTIVITY 2:

A nominal style is not just used by writers of fiction. It can be equally effective in other prose genres. Below is an extract from Walter Pater's *The Renaissance* (1873), in which he describes the effect on the viewer of Leonardo Da Vinci's *La Gioconda* (more popularly known as the Mona Lisa). Why do you think Pater uses so many nouns? Are they effective or redundant? Can you use Ian Watt's comments on a nominal style in prose fiction to identify the effects of Pater's style? Write an analysis of this passage, bearing these questions in mind.

> *La Gioconda* is, in the truest sense, Leonardo's masterpiece, the revealing instance of his mode of thought and work. In its suggestiveness, only the *Melancholia* of Dürer is comparable to it; and no crude symbolism disturbs the effect of its subdued and graceful mystery. We all know the face and hands of the figure, set in its marble chair, in that circle of fantastic rocks, as in some faint light undersea. Perhaps of all ancient pictures time has chilled it least.
>
> The presence that rose thus so strangely beside the waters, is expressive of what in the ways of a thousand years men had come to desire. Hers is the head upon which all 'the ends of the world are come', and the eyelids are a little weary. It is a beauty wrought out from within upon the flesh, the deposit, little cell by cell, of strange thoughts and fantastic reveries and exquisite passions. Set it for a moment beside one of those white Greek goddesses or women of antiquity, and how would they be troubled by this beauty, into which the soul with all its maladies has passed!

> (Pater 1986: 79)

ACTIVITY 3:

Describe in fine detail a room which, for a particular reason, is imprinted on your memory. Use no more than 300 words and draw on what you have learned from Dickens's and Ruskin's nominal style. Aim for compression and focus on description rather than activity within the room.

Passage 2: *Middlemarch* by George Eliot

The passage below from George Eliot's *Middlemarch* (1871–72) presents a scene from married life. Interestingly, the husband is referred to as Mr Casaubon and the wife as Dorothea, supporting Eliot's observation that he was always formal, 'even when he spoke without his waistcoat and cravat'. His reply to Dorothea's expression of concern shows that he cannot or will not change to a colloquial register. Mr Casaubon is much older than Dorothea. She has recently accepted his marriage proposal because she admires his scholarship. She had hoped, as his wife, to share his studies and learn as much as she believes he knows. Their honeymoon in Rome has been a disappointment to her because she feels she was an encumbrance.

> That was an unpropitious hour for coming home: it was too early to gain the moral support under *ennui* of dressing his [Mr Casaubon's] person for dinner, and too late to undress his mind of the day's frivolous ceremony and affairs, so as to be prepared for a good plunge into the serious business of study. On such occasions he usually threw himself into an easy-chair in the library, and allowed Dorothea to read the London papers to him closing his eyes the while. To-day, however, he declined that relief, observing that he already had too many public details urged upon him; but he spoke more cheerfully than usual, when Dorothea asked about his fatigue, and added with the air of formal effort which never forsook him even when he spoke without his waistcoat and cravat –
>
> 'I have had the gratification of meeting my former acquaintance, Dr Spanning, to-day, and of being praised by one who is himself a worthy recipient of praise. He spoke very handsomely of my late tractate on the Egyptian Mysteries, – using, in fact, terms which it would not become me to repeat.' In uttering the last clause, Mr Casaubon leaned over the elbow of his chair, and swayed his head up and down, apparently as a muscular outlet instead of that recapitulation which would not have been becoming.
>
> (Eliot 1871–72: 404)

The grammar of the passage above is fascinating in its use of subject nouns and pronouns. The first paragraph is written in the third person, using Mr Casaubon's full name, or 'he', and only twice referring to Dorothea by name. The main focus is on the husband's thoughts and actions and his control of his wife. The second paragraph comprises Mr Casaubon speaking in the first person and then, after his reply to Dorothea's solicitation, it returns to the third person. At first glance, this would seem to be quite straightforward but the text is much more subtle and revealing when examined in detail. Who would use, for instance, words and phrases such as 'unpropitious', 'ennui', 'frivolous ceremony' and 'observing that he had too many public details urged upon him'? If the pronoun were changed from 'he' to 'I', it could be Mr Casaubon speaking. Therefore, his position and perceptions are implied by the self-regarding formal vocabulary. On the other hand, after the semi-colon, the perspective becomes more objective. The prose moves into comment and interpretation of the kind that George Eliot regularly makes about her characters, not what Mr Casaubon would say about himself. Yet both perspectives are given in the grammatical third person. The prose is sinuous, smoothly changing points of view and drawing attention to what is absent. What, for example, would be Dorothea's account of the conversation with her husband? What would her inner thoughts and choice of language be in comparison with his?

Mr Casaubon's reply to Dorothea is lengthy and pretentious. He does not ask how she is as we might expect from a husband meeting his wife at the end of a day spent going about their separate business. The motive behind Mr Casaubon's words is a desire for compliments; he bathes in the reflective glory of Dr Spanning, who himself is 'a worthy recipient of praise'. Mr Casaubon's diction is markedly latinate, which gives a scholarly air to his pontifications. His sentences have the completed elegance of written language, as if they had been rehearsed and polished, ready for performance before Dorothea. There are no spontaneous or half-finished utterances, which we usually take as indicators of sincerity in the dynamic interaction of conversation. His speech is so self-conscious that we distrust him.

The last sentence of the passage sparkles with caustic wit, presenting Mr Casaubon as ridiculous and pompous. With the passage still in the third person, the perspective has changed from Mr Casaubon's view of himself to the narrator's. By using the grammatical term 'clause', Eliot economically suggests the unnecessary complexity of Mr Casaubon's sentences. This man knows his grammatical subordinates from his co-ordinates! The nodding head, which might in ceremonial circumstances be appropriate, is sanctimonious in a domestic situation. The strongly pejorative adverb 'apparently' exposes the gap between Mr Casaubon's perception of himself as dignified, and Eliot's presentation of him as risible. His solemn body language is reduced, from the author's point of view, to no more than 'a muscular outlet', which she reads as a symptom of self-praise.

The style of the passage displays a superb control of shifting perspectives, enabling the prose to move between various discourses. The focus changes from Mr Casaubon's discourse (both thought and voiced), to authorial voice, and directs itself toward the blank space, the missing voice which belongs to Dorothea. Eliot's style concentrates on the centre, but implies background discourse. Although consistently using third person narration, it has a dialogical (multi-voiced) style.

ACTIVITY 4:

Rewrite the passage from *Middlemarch* using the singular first person pronoun, 'I', writing from the point of view of Dorothea. In other words, write a monologue. Now compare your alternative text with the original, considering the main differences between the two. Rob Pope's observations on the power of pronouns may help you to do this well. He argues that, whether a text uses the grammatical first person (personal), second person (interpersonal) or third person (depersonalised, objective), the position of the other pronouns is implied (Pope 1995: 50–1). He maintains that 'there are potential traces of precisely those other subject positions . . . which at first seemed not to figure in the foreground' (51). You may be able to make use of this idea to identify different discourses, or 'voices', in George Eliot's prose extract and your own rewritten alternative.

Passage 3: *The Waves* by Virginia Woolf

The passage below is an extract from Woolf's novel *The Waves* (1931). The novel is comprised of monologues from six characters who have continued their friendship since childhood. Bernard's monologue below moves back and forth from his inner thoughts to his spoken words, recording his inner and outer experiences of the world as one continuous sequence. He is a writer who 'distrust[s] neat designs of life that are drawn on half-sheets of note-paper' (Woolf 1973: 204). He, perhaps like Woolf, feels that it is all too easy to over-simplify transient and allusive qualities of life when he tries to convey them in his writing.

'And time' said Bernard, 'lets fall its drop. The drop that has formed on the roof of the soul falls. On the roof of my mind time, forming, lets fall its drop. Last week, as I stood shaving, the drop fell. I, standing with my razor in my hand, became suddenly aware of the habitual nature of my action (this is the drop forming) and congratulated my hands, ironically, for keeping at it. Shave, shave, shave, I said. Go on shaving. The drop fell. All through the day's work, at intervals, my mind went to an empty place, saying, "What is lost? What is over?" And "Over and done with," I muttered, "over and done with," solacing myself with words. People noticed the vacuity of my face and the aimlessness of my conversation. The last words of my sentence tailed away. And as I buttoned my coat to go home I said more dramatically, "I have lost my youth."

'It is curious how, at every crisis, some phrase which does not fit insists on coming to the rescue – the penalty of living in an old civilization with a note book. This drop falling has nothing to do with losing my youth. This drop falling is time tapering to a point. Time, which is a sunny pasture covered with a dancing light, time, which is widespread as a field at midday, becomes pendant. Time tapers to a point. As a drop falls from a glass heavy with some sediment, time falls. These are the true cycles, these are the true events. Then as if all the luminosity of the atmosphere were withdrawn I see to the bare bottom. I see what habit covers. I lie sluggish in bed for days. I dine out and gape like a codfish. I do not trouble to finish my sentences, and my actions, usually so uncertain, acquire a mechanical precision. On this occasion, passing an office, I went in and bought, with all the composure of a mechanical figure, a ticket for Rome.'

(Woolf 1973: 157–8)

The passage celebrates the richness of the inner life of the imagination. It shows how gifts of insight are presented to Bernard, often unbidden and often 'hooked out' from the unconscious by the most mundane of daily routines. His daily ritual of shaving, while being a tedious experience in itself, leaves his mind free to wander and to work on the image of a water droplet, thus releasing tenuous associations which eventually form themselves into meaning. On the other hand, the passage shows the struggle through which a writer goes in endeavouring to find the right words to capture the particularity of experience. It suggests that if Bernard can never be satisfied with the words he chooses, then he will be driven to 'an empty place' again and again. The seeds of despair are sown in his initial inspiration, because the passage implies that he may find himself trapped in a continuous cycle of incompletion, and failure to connect with or make any sense of the world outside him.

It would seem at first glance that the passage relies so heavily on the use of metaphor and simile that a grammatical analysis of it would not be particularly fruitful. Yet grammar and syntax have a pervasive effect that intimately connects the subject matter of the passage and its style. For example, in the opening sentences, the cyclical nature of time is imitated in the alternation of subject and direct object. Here, the grammar enacts the meaning. In the first sentence, 'time' is the subject, with 'lets fall' as the verb phrase, and 'drop' as the direct object. Then, in the second sentence, 'drop' becomes the subject and 'falls' the verb. In the third sentence, 'time' reverts to the subject position and 'drop' to the object position. In addition, the verbs 'fall', 'drop' and 'fell' are often delayed to the end of the sentence, making us wait for them and giving a sense of passing time. Thus, in this passage, grammar moves into meaning and the shape of the sentence or the style becomes inseparable from semantics.

ACTIVITY 5:

Virginia Woolf, in her essay 'Modern Fiction' (1925), expressed her belief that novelists should attempt to convey the 'myriad impressions – trivial, fantastic, evanescent, or engraved with the sharpness of steel' which each day brings, otherwise 'life or spirit, truth or reality, this, the essential thing, has moved off or on' (Woolf 1975: 188–9). In retrospect we can recognise her ideas as belonging to the experimental writing of the 1920s, a literary movement which has come to be known as Modernism, but in its time it was unfamiliar advice for a writer of prose fiction. It is easy to see some of Woolf's own characteristics as a writer in her fictional character Bernard, from *The Waves*. Drawing on some of the stylistic and grammatical features of Woolf's writing, write a short passage of about 300 words which captures a fleeting moment of some significance from your own experience, for instance a face seen in a crowd, an image in a dream or a noise you can't quite identify.

ACTIVITY 6:

Compare and contrast the use of language in the passage from Woolf's *The Waves* with the passage below. It is taken from the first volume of Dorothy Richardson's novel *Pilgrimage*, entitled *Pointed Roofs* (1915).

> She got up reluctantly, at the surprise of the very early gonging … Pausing in the bright light of the top landing as Mademoiselle ran down stairs, she had seen through the landing window the deep peak of a distant gable casting an unfamiliar shadow – a shadow sloping the wrong way, a morning shadow. She remembered the first time, the only time, she had noticed such a shadow – getting up early one morning while Harriet and all the household were still asleep – and how she had stopped dressing and gazed at it as it stood there cooler and quiet and alone across the mellow face of a neighbouring stone porch – had suddenly been glad that she was alone and had wondered why that shadowed porch-peak was more beautiful than all the summer things she knew, and had felt at that moment that nothing could touch or trouble her again.
>
> (Richardson 1979: 132)

Here are a few ideas that you might wish to use in order to analyse Woolf's and Richardson's styles. Jane Miller, in her critical book *Women Writing About Men* (1986), praises Dorothy Richardson for perfecting a style of prose in which 'rhythm, intonation, sentence structure and punctuation contribute to a representation of the movement of attention rather than the sequencing of narrative or logic' (187). What do you think she means by this and do you agree? Can you see any points of comparison between this description of Richardson's syntax and the way Woolf constructs her sentences? Write a commentary of about 500 words considering these questions.

Passage 4: *A Maggot* by John Fowles

John Fowles's novel *A Maggot* (1985) begins in an unusual way. There is no chapter number or title, which leaves us adrift and searching for clues to orientate ourselves towards the text. We plunge straight into the opening sentence:

> In the late and last afternoon of an April long ago, a forlorn little group of travellers cross a remote upland in the far south-west of England.

> (Fowles 1986: 7)

This immediately makes us curious and we want to read on. The consonance of the repeated 'l', the rhythmic stress falling on words with an 'l' sound and the phrase 'long ago' all combine to suggest the idiom of a fairy-tale. The sentence economically gives time, setting and characters, but is non-specific. The three indefinite articles imply that we are too far away from the scene to be able to distinguish these people apart as individuals. We have a panoramic view of the landscape and a long-distance view in terms of time. Contrasting with this impression, 'the late and last afternoon of April' is specific and the use of the present tense, which continues throughout the first paragraph, creates a sense of timelessness. The novel has opened with a strong visual image which draws us into the chapter. We want to know the identity of these characters and how they will fit into the forthcoming narrative. John Fowles, in his Prologue to the novel, comments on this image which visited him again and again before he began to develop the narrative in full. He likened it to 'a sequence of looped film in a movie projector; or a single line of verse, the last remnant of a lost myth' (1986: 5). The idea of a film loop captures exactly the sense of suspended time which Fowles has purposely striven for in the opening sentence of the novel. The extract below is the second paragraph. When you read it, ask yourself which elements of style maintain the anonymity of the characters and elicit a feeling of the eternal present.

> A man in his late twenties, in a dark bistre greatcoat, boots and tricorn hat, its upturned edges trimmed discreetly in silver braid, leads the silent caravan. The underparts of his bay, and of his clothes, like those of his companions, are mud-splashed, as if earlier in the day they have travelled in mirier places. He rides with a slack rein and a slight stoop, staring at the track ahead as if he does not see it. Some paces behind comes an older man on a smaller, plumper horse. His greatcoat is in dark grey, his hat black and plainer, and he too looks neither to left or right, but reads a small volume held in his free hand, letting his placid pad tread its own

way. Behind him, on a stouter beast, sit two people: a bare-headed man in a long-sleeved blouse, heavy drugget jerkin and leather breeches, his long hair tied in a knot, with in front of him, sitting sideways and resting against his breast – he supports her back with his right arm – a young woman. She is enveloped in a brown hooded cloak, and muffled so that only her eyes and nose are visible. Behind these two a leading line runs back to a pack-horse. The animal carries a seam, or wooden frame, with a large leather portmanteau tied to one side, and a smaller wooden box, brassbound at its corners, on the other. Various other bundles and bags lie bulkily distributed under a rope net. The overburdened beast plods with hanged head, and sets the pace for the rest.

(Fowles 1986: 7)

The figures in the landscape are anonymous, referred to by general nouns such as 'travellers', 'man', 'woman', 'people', and by personal pronouns. However, their appearance and clothing is minutely described, implying that their individuality is significant and will be revealed in the following chapters. The inscrutable nature of their personalities and motivation is highlighted by the repeated comparative phrase 'as if'. The descriptive style slows down the completion of the sentences, adding to an impression of slow movement. The main verbs are often placed well into the sentences. For example, in the first sentence of the novel, the main verb, 'cross', sits in the middle. It has an adverbial phrase of time branching to its left, and the subject word, 'group', modified by pre- and post-modifying adjectival phrases, branching to its right and to its left. The first sentence of the printed extract begins with the subject, 'A man', and continues with embedded adjectival phrases until it arrives at the main verb, 'leads'. In both cases, there is a delay before reaching the verb, so the style imitates the slow movement of the travellers. The rhythm of the sentences is enacting the meaning. The verbs themselves, the words which signify movement, are 'moving slowly'.

The prepositional phrases – 'Some paces behind', 'Behind him' and 'Behind these' – are evenly spaced in this text and also mark out the slow sequence of movement. They come at the beginning of sentences, which emphasises their importance, and in two cases immediately precede the main verbs. A prepositional phrase, followed by the main verb ('come' and 'sit'), followed by the subject of the verb ('an older man' and 'two people'), inverts the normal word order of a clause and introduces another grammatical strategy for creating the impression of perpetual motion. The alliterated 'b's in the last two sentences evoke a feeling of heaviness and weariness as the overladen pack horse struggles on. The sentence, in tandem with the horse, 'plods' in slow rhythms to the end of the paragraph. This analysis shows that Fowles has used many stylistic devices in this passage in order to achieve its visual and dynamic effects, but underlying all of them is grammar and syntax.

ACTIVITY 7:

Maintaining as far as possible the same style, write a third paragraph following on from the passage above, or write a parody of this passage in the style of a 'Spaghetti' Western. Remember to maintain the anonymity of the cowboys and to keep your reader guessing which character is the Clint Eastwood figure! Or rewrite the passage, introducing suitable dialogue and using verb tenses that place events in the past. Write a commentary on the difference in stylistic effect between your version and the original passage and on the grammatical choices you made in order to achieve this effect.

Passage 5: *Under Milk Wood* by Dylan Thomas

The fifth passage for analysis is an interesting one, because it was written for radio. Its writer, Dylan Thomas, was born in Swansea and lived near The Mumbles which he probably used as a model for Milk Wood, for a large part of his life. Consequently, the rhythms of *Under Milk Wood* are heavily influenced by the lyricism of the Welsh accent. Thomas is famous, or infamous, for his inspirational, drunken poetry-readings in America before his death in 1953. His fascination, not to say obsession, with the sound of words and the cadence of phrases and sentences shows itself in his prose as well as his poetry. The extract below is taken from the opening sequence, when the First Voice describes the Welsh villagers and village of Milk Wood, spread out before the listening audience's imagination.

> Listen. It is night in the chill, squat chapel, hymning, in bonnet and brooch and bombazine black, butterfly choker and bootlace bow, coughing like nannygoats, sucking mintoes, fortywinking hallelujah; night in the four-ale, quiet as a dominoe; in Ocky Milkman's loft like a mouse with gloves; in Dai Bread's bakery flying like black flour. It is tonight in Donkey street, trotting silent, with seaweed on its hooves, along the cockled cobbles, past curtained fernpot, text and trinket, harmonium, holy dresser, watercolours, done by hand, china dog and rosy tin teacaddy. It is night neddying among the snuggeries of babies.
>   Look. It is night, dumbly, royally winding through the Coronation cherry trees; going through the graveyard of Bethesda with winds gloved and folded, and dew doffed; tumbling by the Sailors' Arms.
>   Time passes. Listen. Time passes.
>   Come closer now.
>   Only you can hear the houses sleeping in the streets in the slow deep salt and silent black, bandaged night. Only you can see, in the blinded bedrooms, the coms and petticoats over the chairs, the jugs and basins, the

glasses of teeth, Thou Shalt Not on the wall, and the yellowing dickybird-watching pictures of the dead. Only you can hear and see, behind the eyes of the sleepers, the movements and countries and mazes and colours and dismays and rainbows and tunes and wishes and flight and fall and despairs and big seas of their dreams.

From where you are, you can hear their dreams.

(Thomas 1995: 4)

The style of this passage is effective in many ways. The first feature that is striking is its sleepy rhythm in the long and short sentences, which is most appropriate to the subject of a village asleep. Secondly, the First Voice addresses us directly, drawing us into the radio play, urging us to enter the village and inviting us to meet its fictional inhabitants. Thirdly, the First Voice takes us on an imaginary journey, moving from a view of the streets and buildings of the village, into the houses, rooms and bedrooms of the villagers, and lastly, into the intimate spaces of their dreams.

How does Dylan Thomas achieve these effects? What grammatical and syntactical strategies does he use to create such textual richness? Rhythm is partly created by the contrast of sentence length. This is particularly important for a listening audience or a reader who 'listens' with an inner ear. The short sentences – 'Listen', 'Look' and 'Come closer now' – all use commands (imperatives). These have the effect of creating a seemingly direct relationship between the writer and the reader. In addition, the text encourages us to make use of other senses besides listening by often placing the words 'listen', 'hear', 'look' and 'see' close together. The repeated imperatives provide structure and cohesion to an otherwise fluid and flowing text. They are signposts which operate by sound and rhythm, as well as meaning.

The long sentences also have repeated grammatical patterns. Those of the first half of the passage all begin with 'It is night' (or 'It is tonight'). This simple sentence, made up of a subject pronoun (It), a present tense verb (is), and a complement (night), is like a repeated refrain in a song. Because the present tense is used and because the repetition introduces pacing, there is a feeling of continuous and slow passing time.

The repeated simple sentences all have long strings of prepositional phrases, adverbial phrases and non-finite clauses dependent upon them. These always branch to the right of 'it is night', that is, they always follow rather than precede the 'kernel' or main clause. Once we have noticed this pattern, we await its repetition. Thus, the prose has a rocking, halt-and-release effect. In the second section of the passage, a similar syntactical pattern emerges which has an equally soporific rocking sound. In this second section, the main clause, with variations, is 'Only you can hear/see/hear and see'. Once again, strings of phrases hang on to the kernel sentence. Thus the prose style is in tune with the meaning of the passage, because the slow passing of time is enacted in the syntax and rhythms of the sentences.

By using the adverb 'only' in conjunction with the pronoun 'you', the passage is welcoming and creates a feeling of exclusivity for us. Dylan Thomas invites us to peep into his characters' dreams. The rhythms of the prose change once the text moves from the sleepers' bedrooms into their fantasies. The repeated use of the co-ordinating conjunction 'and', twelve times in a row, indicates the slow motion and expansiveness of their dreams. The last sentence flows along without restraint and is beautifully balanced.

This analysis has concentrated on the grammatical and syntactical basis of Thomas's style. If you were undertaking a more wide-ranging stylistic analysis we might have considered the visual images that the passage creates and the figures of speech that it uses. Defining and separating these different features of language is a necessary activity for us here but in practice all of these elements of style work closely together and strengthen each other.

ACTIVITY 8:

Delete all of the adjectives in the passage. This includes all adjectives positioned before the noun as pre-modifiers, nouns which function as adjectives pre-modifying other nouns, adjectives placed after the noun and adjectival phrases. Now compare the original passage and the passage with deletions. Write 300 words describing what is lost or gained by deletion in your rewritten version and give reasons for your opinion. Here is an idea that may be useful to you in this activity. As we mentioned in Chapter 4, F.R. Leavis criticised Joseph Conrad for 'adjectival insistence' in his novel *Heart of Darkness*. In short, according to Leavis, Conrad used so many adjectives that the effect was 'not to magnify, but rather to muffle' (Leavis 1966: 196–7). Do you think this criticism could be made against Dylan Thomas's prose, or do his strings of adjectives have some purpose, the loss of which would diminish the passage?

ACTIVITY 9:

Below is one of the passages by Joseph Conrad to which Leavis refers in *The Great Tradition*. The narrator of this extract from *The Heart of Darkness* (1899), Marlow, was sent to the Belgian Congo to search out a colonial administrator, Mr Kurtz. Kurtz had gone to Africa as a high-minded educator and had ended as the god of a head-hunting tribe. He dies mysteriously uttering the phrase 'The horror! The horror!' On his return from the Congo, Marlow is faced with the necessity of lying to Kurtz's fiancée about the circumstances of Kurtz's death. Write a 300-word critical analysis of the style of the passage and consider whether Leavis's comments on 'adjectival insistence' are valid here.

She came forward, all in black, with a pale head, floating towards me in the dusk. She was in mourning. It was more than a year since his [Mr Kurtz's] death, more than a year since the news came; she seemed as though she would remember and mourn for ever. She took both my hands in hers and murmured, 'I heard you were coming.' I noticed she was not very young – I mean not girlish. She had a mature capacity for fidelity, for belief, for suffering. The room seemed to have grown darker, as if all the sad light of the cloudy evening had taken refuge on her forehead. This fair hair, this pale visage, this pure brow, seemed surrounded by a halo from which the dark eyes looked out at me. Their glance was guileless, profound, confident, and trustful. She carried her sorrowful head as though she were proud of that sorrow, as though she would say, I – I alone know how to mourn for him as he deserves. But while we were still shaking hands, such a look of awful desolation came upon her face that I perceived she was one of those creatures that are not the playthings of Time. For her he had died only yesterday. And, by Jove! The impression was so powerful that for me, too, he seemed to have died only yesterday – nay, this very minute. I saw her and him in the same instant of time – his death and her sorrow – I saw her sorrow in the very moment of death. Do you understand? I saw them together – I heard them together. She said, with a deep catch of the breath, 'I have survived' while my strained ears seemed to hear distinctly, mingled with her tone of despairing regret, the summing up whisper of his eternal condemnation. I asked myself what I was doing there, with a sensation of panic in my heart as though I had blundered into a place of cruel and absurd mysteries not fit for a human being to behold.

(Conrad 1982: 106–7)

Passage 6: 'The Colonel' by Carolyn Forché

The sixth passage, which is set in Latin America, could not be more different from Dylan Thomas's *Under Milk Wood*. When you begin reading the text below, ask yourself whether its style corresponds to its meaning, and if so, how? It is, in fact, taken from a collection of poems. Why do you think the poet has chosen to write in prose to present this particular experience?

What you have heard is true. I was in his house. His wife carried a tray of coffee and sugar. His daughter filed her nails, his son went out for the night. There were daily papers, pet dogs, a pistol on the cushion beside him. The moon swung bare on its black cord over the house. On the television was a cop show. It was in English. Broken bottles were embedded in the walls of the house to scoop the kneecaps from a man's legs or cut his hands to lace. On the window there were gratings like those in liquor stores. We had dinner, rack of lamb, good wine, a gold bell was on the table for calling the maid. The maid brought green mangoes, salt, a type of bread. I was asked how I enjoyed the country. There was a brief commercial in Spanish. His wife took everything away. There was some talk then about how difficult it had become to govern. The parrot said hello on the terrace. The colonel told it to shut up, and pushed himself from the table. My friend said to me with his eyes: say nothing. The colonel returned with a sack used to bring groceries home. He spilled many human ears on the table. They were like dried peach halves. There is no other way to say this. He took one of them in his hands, shook it in our faces, dropped it into a water glass. It came alive there. I am tired of fooling around, he said. As for the rights of anyone, tell your people they can go f– themselves. He swept the ears to the floor with his arm and held the last of his wine in the air. Something for your poetry, no? he said. Some of the ears on the floor caught the scrap of his voice. Some of the ears were pressed to the ground.

(Forché 1992: 225)

This grammatically 'simple' piece of writing is shocking in its presentation of human callousness and the abuse of political and military power. Its effects are produced, in part, by the horrific action of the Colonel, as he spills a grocery sack of human ears onto the table where a family and guests have just eaten a very civilised meal. The horror of this event is strengthened by its unexpected eruption into a familiar 'normal' domestic scene. The event also underlines the habitual cruelty of the Colonel, who wines and dines his guests and then verbally intimidates them with such panache. One guest, the narrator, is a poet, and yet she or he deliberately suppresses poetic writing in the name of factual truth. We can see this in the opening sentence as s/he verifies 'What you have heard is true'. S/he sounds reluctant or apologetic about reporting such an atrocious act, as s/he explains 'There is no other way to say this'. As if giving testimony in a court of law, the narrator's manner of delivery is low key, restricting itself to a factual account of what happened and who said what. This makes the metaphors in the last two sentences movingly resonant. They suddenly invigorate the whole passage, showing that the Colonel had not managed to annihilate the spirit of his guest, and hinting that underground resistance also has not been eradicated.

So how does the syntax of the sentences in this passage underpin its presentation of controlled and calculated violence against human beings? Sentences are either grammatically simple (one-clause) or co-ordinated but often with the connective left out. The function of co-ordination is to indicate that each sentence or phrase is of equal grammatical value, and, by implication, of equal value in its meaning (semantic value). Co-ordination also suggests that there is no cause and effect, connection or relationship between what is expressed in one sentence and what is expressed in the next. Therefore, in this passage, it initially comes as a surprise when we read that 'daily papers, pet dogs, a pistol' lie together on a cushion beside the Colonel. This close proximity of the domestic and the sadistic becomes a repeated pattern, increasing in intensity throughout the passage, leading to the final horror of spilling the dried ears on the table, 'like dried peach halves'. The unlikely yoking together of ears and peaches increases the effect of the grotesque.

The co-ordinated sentence structure persists throughout. One resulting stylistic effect of this is understatement. The co-ordination remains constant, while the content becomes more gruesome. Consequently, divergence between style and meaning becomes ironic, emphasising the extreme horror of the situation. On the other hand, the co-ordinated style is appropriate to the Colonel's perception of his world. We can see that for him, government by terror and torture is quite 'normal', as normal as eating supper and drinking wine. The style, therefore, points out two different points of view of host and guest. Moreover, the lack of conjunctions and subordinated clauses creates a fictional world in which nothing appears to connect with anything else. Such a world, which cannot be fathomed or predicted except in its random perpetration of violence, would indeed be a terrifying world. The co-ordinated style, therefore, contributes towards the feeling in the passage of vulnerability. It helps us to imagine what it must be like to live in a world where we cannot link our experiences by cause and effect and where we might be violated at any time.

ACTIVITY 10:

Rewrite the passage, inserting connectives between the simple sentences. Use both co-ordinating and subordinating conjunctions, phrases, and whole sentences if necessary, in order to show relationships, in terms of time, place or cause, between the original passage's disparate sentences. Write about 300 words comparing the original passage with your expanded version. Describe what effect your additions have had, giving some thought to whether your connectives improve the passage, change its meaning or are redundant. Here is a comment on prose style which may be a useful insight into the function of connectives. In an essay on Jonathan Swift's style, Louis Milic makes the point that Swift uses connectives copiously, sometimes two or three at a time, as in 'and although' or 'and likewise because' (Milic 1970: 252). He concludes that, by this means, Swift creates an illusion of clarity and persuasiveness, whereas actually, his use of connectives 'show[s] only that one sentence is connected to another without reference to the nature of the connection' (247). Can you use this critical comment on Swift's writing to explore the effects of the connectives that you have inserted into your rewriting of Forché's text?

ACTIVITY 11:

The passage below is an extract from Jonathan Swift's *A Modest Proposal* (1729). It is a political satire that belongs to a specific historical period and place. In 1722, the currency in Ireland was devalued through the introduction of copper coinage authorised by the English Treasury. The patent was revoked in 1725, but only after the coins had flooded the country and increased widespread poverty. Swift was outraged at the treatment of the Irish by the landlords of the English Ascendency and the government. He was also embittered by his perceived 'banishment' from England to a Deanship in Ireland. This led him to write scathing political pamphlets. His *Drapier's Letters* (1724–25) attacked the introduction of the copper coinage (nicknamed Wood's Halfpenny after the hardware dealer who minted them); *A Modest Proposal* followed, addressing with vitriol the problem of starvation among the Irish populace. Bearing in mind Milic's comments on Swift's use of connectives to join his sentences and clauses together, analyse how Swift contrives to make his abominable proposal sound so logical and persuasive. The connectives, which are of various kinds, have been italicised in the passage.

I shall now *therefore* humbly propose my own thoughts, *which* I hope will not be lyable to the least Objection.

I have been assured by a very knowing American of my acquaintance in London, *that* a young healthy Child well Nursed is at a year Old a most delicious, nourishing, and wholesome, Food, whether Stewed, Roasted, Baked, or Boyled, *and* I make no doubt *that* it will equally serve in a Fricasie, or a Ragout.

I do *therefore* humbly offer it to publick consideration *that* of the hundred and twenty thousand Children, already computed, twenty thousand may be reserved for Breed, whereof only one fourth part to be Males, which is more than we allow to Sheep, black Cattle, or Swine, *and* my reason is *that* these Children are seldom the Fruits of Marriage, a Circumstance not much regarded by our savages, *therefore* one Male will be sufficient to serve four Females. *That* the remaining hundred thousand may at a year Old be offered in Sale to the persons of Quality, and Fortune, through the Kingdom, always advising the Mother to let them Suck plentifully in the last Month, *so as* to render them Plump, and Fat for a good Table. A Child will make two Dishes at an Entertainment for Friends, *and when* the Family dines alone, the fore or hind Quarter will make a reasonable Dish, *and* seasoned with a little Pepper or Salt will be very good Boiled on the fourth Day, especially in Winter.

I grant this food will be somewhat dear, *and therefore* very proper for Landlords, *who*, *as* they have already devoured most of the Parents, seem to have the best Title to the Children.

(Swift 1963: 514–15)

Summary

The purpose of this chapter has been to give you the opportunity to:

- consolidate your recognition of various aspects of grammar
- analyse the effects of grammatical features on style
- consider the close, reinforcing connection between grammar and style
- define style by examining sentence structure
- compare prose styles
- practise writing different varieties of prose and writing creatively.

References

Conrad, Joseph (1977) *'The Nigger of The "Narcissus"'*, *'Typhoon' and Other Stories* [1897]. Harmondsworth: Penguin.

Conrad, Joseph (1982) *Heart of Darkness* [1899]. Harmondsworth: Penguin.

Dickens, Charles (1953) *Great Expectations* [1861]. London: Collins.

Eagleton, Mary (1990) *Feminist Literary Theory* [1986]. Oxford: Blackwell.

Eliot, George (1996) *Middlemarch* [1871–72]. Harmondsworth: Penguin.

Forché, Carolyn (1992) 'The Colonel' (1982) in M. Peet and D. Robinson (eds), *Leading Questions*. Walton-on-Tharnes: Nelson.

Fowles, John (1986) *A Maggot* [1985]. London: Pan.

Freeman, D.C. (ed.) (1970) *Linguistics and Literary Style*. Massachusetts: Massachusetts University Press.

Leavis, F.R. (1983) *The Great Tradition* [1948]. Harmondsworth: Penguin.

Milic, L.T. (1970) 'Connectives in Swift's Prose Style' in D.C. Freeman (ed.), *Linguistics and Literary Style*. Massachusetts: Massachusetts University Press.

Miller, Jane (1986) *Women Writing About Men*. London: Virago.

Pater, W. (1986) *The Renaissance* [1873]. Oxford: Oxford University Press.

Pope, Rob (1995) *Textual Interventions*. London: Routledge.

Richardson, Dorothy (1979) *Pilgrimage 1* [1915–17]. Illinois: Illinois University Press.

Swift, Jonathan (1963) *A Modest Proposal* [1729] in J. Hayward (ed.), *Jonathan Swift*. London: Nonesuch.

Thomas, Dylan (1995) *Under Milk Wood* [1954]. London: Dent.

Watt, Ian (1957) *The Rise of the Novel: Studies in Defoe, Richardson and Fielding*. London: Chatto & Windus.

Weldon, Fay (1984) *Letters to Alice: On First Reading Jane Austen*. London: Sceptre.

Woolf, Virginia (1973) *The Waves* [1931]. Harmondsworth: Penguin.

Woolf, Virginia (1975) *The Common Reader* [1925]. London: Hogarth.

Woolf, Virginia (1993) *A Room of One's Own* [1929]. London: Flamingo.

Trouble-shooting: Twelve common grammatical errors in writing

Peter Chapman

I n this final section we have collected together twelve common grammatical errors in order to show you how to recognise and correct them in your own writing. Knowledge you have acquired working through this book will help here – particularly knowledge about punctuation, the difference between independent and dependent clauses, and the relationship between subject and verb elements.

Agreement (concord)

Neither of the following sentences is grammatically correct but one seems obviously more acceptable than the other. Do you agree?

> My daughter do her homework after supper.
> The change in people's attitudes to drink-driving are encouraging.

The first sentence would be acceptable in Suffolk regional speech, for instance, but not in Standard English because the combination of a singular subject ('My daughter') and a plural verb ('do') does not work.

Rules at work here:

Subject and verb should agree or 'match up' in number.
It is the number of the head word in the subject noun phrase which determines the number of the verb.

All the forms of the verb 'to do' in the present tense are 'do' except for the third person singular, 'does'. So the correct version is:

> My daughter does her homework after supper.

The second sentence is also unacceptable in Standard English because the subject and verb forms do not agree in number. The subject is singular ('change') but the verb is plural ('are encouraging'). The verb should be singular ('is encouraging') to match the subject. There is more chance of a mistake being made here because of the long noun phrase ('The change in people's attitudes to drink-driving') which is acting as the subject of the verb. This creates a distance between the head word of the noun phrase ('change') and the verb. Also the plural noun 'attitudes' is closer to the verb and may have made the writer think that the verb needed to be in the plural.

The rule then is that it is the number of the head word in the subject noun phrase which determines the number of the verb. For example:

> The *things* you say to your boss *seem* a bit rude to me.

The head word 'things' needs the plural verb 'seem' (it seems, they seem) to achieve agreement.

Sometimes, however, the meaning of a subject can override its number. Compare, for example, the following pairs of sentences:

> Five miles is a long way to walk.
> Law and order is important to this Government.

> Five men are coming to mend the roof.
> Law and order are both important to this government.

In the first two sentences, the plural noun phrase is thought of as a single idea and should therefore have a singular verb, whereas in the second pair this is not the case.

Finally, there needs to be agreement in number between nouns or pronouns in the subject and the object expressions of a clause. For example,

> My daughters do *their* homework after supper.
> *They* are going to be good doctors.
> *We* really must sort out *our* bookshelves.

Note that the grammatical principle of agreement can also be called concord.

Dangling participles

The following sentences consist of a non-finite clause and a main clause, but something has gone wrong in each of them:

> Reading *Wuthering Heights*, Heathcliff never fails to make an impression.
> Walking along the river bank, the evening air gave us a relaxed and contented feeling.

These sentences are unsatisfactory because the *implied subject* of the non-finite clause, 'Reading *Wuthering Heights*', 'Walking along the river bank', and the *explicit subject* of the main clauses do not match up, producing an effect of dislocated (and absurd) meaning. For instance,in the first sentence, it seems to be Heathcliff who is reading *Wuthering Heights*, and in the second, the evening air which is taking the walk! Check this for yourself.

> **Rule at work here:**
>
> Participles should be firmly attached to the main clause.

The participle (the '–ing' and '–ed' forms) is said to be 'dangling' because it is not firmly attached, grammatically, to the main clause. You can rectify such errors by checking that your non-finite clauses are attached to your main clause like this:

> Reading *Wuthering Heights*, I was struck by the impressive character of Heathcliff. (Who was reading *Wuthering Heights*? I was.)
> Walking along the river bank, we were delighted by the relaxing evening air. (Who was walking along the river bank? We were.)

Here is another example from a student essay on Stanley Kubrick's film *Dr Strangelove*:

> Released in 1964, during the heightened military aggression between America and Vietnam, Kubrick engages with the audience's fear of escalation towards nuclear war.

As it stands, the sentence sets up the implication that Kubrick was released in 1964, which is clearly nonsensical. Simply replace 'Kubrick' with

'Kubrick's film' and the sentence becomes grammatically well-formed and makes good sense.

Here are three more sentences with dangling participles in the non-finite clause. Work out what it would take to correct them:

> Travelling to the theatre, the bus broke down.
> Reading my essay through, a number of mistakes needed correction.
> Studied with care, I find Shakespeare's *Hamlet* very interesting.

Faulty parallelism

In the following sentence grammatical consistency has been lost, with the result that the meaning is less clear than it might be. You will probably have to read the sentence at least twice to grasp the connection between its units and the overall meaning:

> The politician's aims include winning the election, a national health programme and the education system.

'Parallelism' means using the same structure for units of meaning which have the same role in a sentence or clause.

Rule at work here:

Parallel grammatical units in formal writing should share the same grammatical structure

---

In the above sentence, the writer lists the politician's aims after the verb 'include' so each of these aims is acting as the object of the verb. Each needs to be expressed with the same structure. The first of the three aims stated is in the form of a non-finite clause ('winning the election'), so the following two aims should also be in this form if the sentence is going to make clear sense. (After all a politician's *aim* cannot be 'an education system' or 'the national health service'.) The corrected sentence might read:

> The politician's aims include *winning* the election, *strengthening* the national health service and *improving* the education system.

What changes could be made to rectify the following unsatisfactory sentence? Here we are dealing not with a list but a contrast of ideas:

> Some commentators are not so much opposed to capital punishment but they want to postpone it for a period of time.

The units in this structure ('Some commentators are not so much A but B') are not parallel; 'opposed to capital punishment' is not parallel to 'they want to postpone it'. There is nothing wrong with 'it' standing in for capital punishment in the second unit but the switch from the use of the –ed participle ('opposed') to pronoun and finite verb ('they want') is very awkward and grammatically incorrect. Here is an improvement in consistency and clarity:

> Some commentators are not so much *opposed* to capital punishment as *committed* to postponing it for a period of time.

Incomplete sentences

Why is the second sentence in the following pair not well-formed?

> Many people have to put up with hard tap water. For example, most of the South East and the West Midlands.

The second sentence contains an adverbial ('for example') and a lengthy noun phrase ('most of the South East and the West Midlands'), but there is no finite verb phrase which means that a most important clause element has been left out. 'Incomplete sentences' are those which lack the essential elements of a clause, usually either a subject element or a verb element.

Rule at work here:

Normally, every complete sentence in formal writing should have at least a subject element and a verb element.

To correct the sentence above we have to add a finite verb phrase and anything else that the verb requires such as an object if the verb takes an object:

For example, most of the residents of the South East and the West Midlands *fall into this category.*

Here is another example of an incomplete sentence:

Putting enough water in the kettle early in the morning for several cups of tea.

This is quite a lengthy string of words containing several units of meaning, but nothing can disguise the fact that it is a non-finite clause ('putting' is a participle and therefore has no person, number or tense) and so the 'sentence' lacks a main clause to make completed meaning. Here are two ways of rectifying the mistake:

Putting enough water in the kettle early in the morning for several cups of tea *makes a good start to the day.*
Putting enough water in the kettle early in the morning for several cups of tea *is important if you are going to have a well-organised morning routine.*

Awareness of the contrast between independent and dependent clauses (Chapter 1) and the essential elements of clauses (Chapter 2) will be a guard against producing incomplete sentences – or, if you inadvertently produce them, will ensure that you are able to see what has gone wrong.

Who/whom

What grammatical considerations affect the choice of 'who' or 'whom' in the following sentences?

The character who crosses the stage at this point is the male lead in the play.
The character who I most identify with is Hamlet.

In speech 'who' would almost certainly be acceptable in both sentences. Also, 'that' could be used instead of 'who' in both sentences and 'who' can be left out in the second sentence but not the first. Try this out. This last feature gives us a clue to the grammatical difference between the two sentences which most people would say needs to be observed in formal writing.

> **Rule at work here:**
>
> 'Who' is the subject position form and 'whom' is the object position form of the relative pronoun.

This can be demonstrated by asking: who crossed the stage? The character (subject) crossed the stage. Who do I identify with? I (subject) identify with Hamlet (object). The object position of the relative pronoun is 'whom'; so the second sentence needs to be changed to 'whom I identify with'.

> The character whom I identify with is Hamlet.

Furthermore, to be fully formal in style, the preposition 'with' needs to be moved into line with the relative pronoun it complements:

> The character with whom I identify is Hamlet.

This construction is common in formal writing: 'in whom', 'for whom', 'by whom', 'from whom', 'to whom' etc.

Here is a practical guideline: if 'who' is followed by a verb then it remains 'who' (subject position), but if it is followed by a noun or personal pronoun ('I', 'you', 'she', etc.) then 'whom' is preferred.

> There are few people at the court in whom Hamlet can confide.
> The writer and critic to whom we all owe a debt of thanks is Virginia Woolf.
> The writer whom we all admire is Shakespeare.

Fewer/less

Are the following sentences acceptable?

> I listen to *less* records now than I used to.
> You really ought to take *less* sugar in your tea.
> He made *less* mistakes than most people.

> **Rule at work:**
>
> The rule here is that 'few/fewer/fewest' are the adjectives that match up with countable nouns and 'little/less/least' with non-countable nouns (e.g. money, sugar, milk).

So the answer is that the first and the third of these sentences need alteration to 'fewer records' and 'fewer mistakes'.

The same conclusion occurs with the superlative forms of 'little' and 'few' as in the following:

> He is the one who makes the least mistakes.
> ('fewest mistakes' is correct because mistakes are countable)
> You should take the least notes possible at this meeting.
> ('fewest notes' is correct because notes are countable)

Apostrophes

Anyone who has worked carefully through Chapter 5 should have no difficulty in seeing what is wrong in each of the following sentences:

> 1. Her shoe's are completely wet through.
> 2. He read's very fluently for a seven-year-old.
> 3. I do hope you find that its not too late.
> 4. It is the Councils responsibility to care for the elderly.
> 5. The banking system may need improving but it's value to the country is not in doubt.

Part of the reason why mistakes like these are made is that all words ending in 's' in speech *sound* the same (e.g. 'its' and 'it's'). But the final 's' in each of the above key words is making a different grammatical contribution to that word. The function of 's' in each sentence above is as follows:

1. The 's' here forms the plural of regular nouns like shoe, book, house etc. No apostrophe is needed.
2. The 's' here forms the third person singular of the present tense of the verb. No apostrophe is needed.
3. The 's' is the remaining letter of the word 'is' when the words 'it' and 'is' are contracted in informal language. It should read 'it's too late'. An apostrophe *is* needed.
4. The 's' here should function to indicate a possessive: 'the Council's responsibility'. An apostrophe is needed to indicate the possessive.
5. The 's' here is the last letter of the possessive pronoun 'its' which is on a par with 'his', 'her', 'your', 'their' etc. and should not be confused with the contracted form 'it's' meaning 'it is'. No apostrophe is needed.

Awareness of whether a final 's' is contributing to a plural form, a contracted form or a possessive form will tell you whether to use an apostrophe or not.

Comma splices

What is wrong with the use of commas in the following sentences?:

> In 1952 Japan's GNP was one third that of France, by the late 1970s it was larger than the GNPs of France and Britain combined.
> The government was defeated, this led to an early election.

The term 'comma splice' refers to the use of a comma between two independent clauses. Commas cannot be used between independent clauses. The result is usually that the use of the comma suggests that the two independent clauses are not independent but in fact connected. 'Splice', then, means 'a join', but in this case a 'bad join' between independent clauses.

> **Rule at work here:**
>
> There are three acceptable ways of marking the relationship between independent clauses (see Chapter 5): a full stop, a semi-colon or a co-ordinating conjunction.

So, you can usually fix the error by changing the comma to a full stop, making the two clauses into two separate sentences, or by changing the comma to a semi-colon. Or you can make one clause dependent.

> Incorrect: I like this book, it is very funny.
> Correct: I like this book. It is very funny.
> (or) I like this book and it is very funny.
> (or) I like this book; it is very funny.
> (or) I like this book because it is very funny.
> (or) Because it is very funny, I like this book.

Avoidance of comma splices depends on being aware of the difference between independent and dependent clauses.

Pronouns and male bias in writing

Most people these days accept that male bias in language should be avoided wherever possible. It is therefore understandable that there is a tendency for people to use the following constructions:

The reader quickly realises that *they* are being asked to consider some difficult issues.
Anyone who wishes to apply for the course should send *their* details to the course organiser.
The customer should ask *themselves* several questions.

In the first common mistake listed above, we pointed out that pronouns and nouns used in different clause elements need to agree. The problem in the above sentences is that, to avoid male bias, the writer has combined a singular pronoun or noun phrase with a plural possessive pronoun.

The reader (singular) . . . they (plural)
Anyone (singular) . . . their (plural)
The customer (singular) . . . themselves (plural)

David Crystal states that such a strategy has become acceptable in informal but not in formal usage because 'it goes against the general practice of Standard English' (Crystal 1996: 157). So, how can we avoid male bias but still remain true to the principles of Standard English? There are a number of current options, none of them problem-free:

- Some academics write 'she' when traditionally 'he' would have been expected ('The reader quickly realises that she is being asked to consider some difficult questions'). This 'reverse discrimination' has not proved acceptable to everyone and remains unusual.
- Some writers invent a sex-neutral/gender-neutral pronoun to use where no distinction between men and women is intended. The new form 's/he' is in widespread use in writing but can only be used when the word order of a clause makes it possible. This would suit the first of the above sentences, but not the other two, for instance.
- Some writers use both third person singular pronouns 'he or she'/'he and she'. Many people find this formula acceptable.
- Many writers change the construction by making the initial noun or pronouns plural. For example:

Readers quickly realise that *they* are being asked to consider some difficult issues. *Those* who wish to apply for the course should send *their* details to the course organiser.

'Neither is' . . . or 'either are'

We used the word 'Neither' at the beginning of the first trouble-shooting section. The next feature of written language that we wish to draw your attention to is the grammar of that very word and others like it such as 'each', 'anybody' and 'none'. The problem they cause some people stems from uncertainty about whether they are singular or plural. Here are some examples of sentences in which these words have caused a confusion between singular and plural:

Neither John nor David *come* to class on Fridays.
Each person must make sure that *they* arrive on time.
Anybody who wishes to attend the meeting should sign *their* name on the list.
None of the books I have read *are* relevant.

> **Rule at work here:**
>
> Formal usage requires that each of the above lead words should be followed by verbs and pronouns in the singular. 'Anybody', 'neither', 'each' and 'none' are all singular forms.

This seems most obvious perhaps in the case of 'each' and least obvious in the case of 'none': 'each' seems logically to imply separate individuals, whereas 'none' seems to have a collective meaning. However, 'none' needs to be understood as 'not one' and so requires to be followed by singular verbs and pronouns. Formal usage therefore requires the following:

Neither John nor David *comes* to class on Fridays.
Each person must make sure that *s/he* arrives on time.
Anybody who wishes to attend the meeting should sign *his or her* name on the list.
None of the books I have read *is* relevant.

Missing comma after a parenthesis

A parenthesis is a piece of information inserted into a sentence that is grammatically complete without it. This information can be marked off from the rest of the sentence by dashes, brackets or commas, although the most commonly used punctuation for the following kind of parenthesis is the comma:

> John – the gardener's brother – felt strongly about delphiniums.
> John (the gardener's brother) felt strongly about delphiniums.
> *John, the gardener's brother, felt strongly about delphiniums.*

A common error in punctuation is to miss out the second of the two delineating commas, like this:

> John, the gardener's brother felt strongly about delphiniums.

Missing out the comma (or dash or bracket) confuses the meaning of the sentence.

Misuse of commas in defining information

A final common punctuation error is one in which a piece of defining information is incorrectly separated off from the rest of the sentence by commas (i.e. as a parenthesis). Here is an example:

> Dickens's novel, *The Mystery of Edwin Drood*, was unfinished at his death.

Separating off '*The Mystery of Edwin Drood*' as a parenthesis implies that it is a *non-defining* piece of information that could be omitted from the sentence without altering the meaning. This would be the case if *The Mystery of Edwin Drood* were the only novel by Dickens. But in fact the title of the novel is essential to the sense of the sentence: it is *defining* information. The sentence should therefore read:

> Dickens's novel *The Mystery of Edwin Drood* was unfinished at his death.

This implies, correctly, that *The Mystery of Edwin Drood* is one of several novels by Dickens, and it is specifically *this one* that was unfinished.

The following sentence is also correct:

> Dickens's final novel, *The Mystery of Edwin Drood*, was unfinished at his death.

In this case, the addition of 'final' changes '*The Mystery of Edwin Drood*' into non-defining information (i.e. there was only one *final* novel). Removing it would not alter the meaning of the sentence. Hence it can be added as a parenthesis.

Reference

Crystal, David (1996) *Rediscover Grammar*. Harlow: Longman.

GLOSSARY

Tory Young and Rebecca Stott

active/passive voice   In the active voice the subject has an active relationship with the verb and does the acting (e.g. The dog ate my homework). In the passive voice the subject has a passive relationship with the verb and is acted upon (e.g. My homework was eaten by the dog).

adjective   Words that modify nouns by adding to their meanings (e.g. That was a *long* film). Most adjectives have comparative (I'm glad it wasn't any *longer*) and superlative forms (It was the *longest* film I've ever seen).

adverb   Single words that modify verbs by adding to their meanings (e.g. The choir sang *sweetly*).

adverbial   Words or phrases that modify or give extra definition to the verb in terms of place, manner and time (e.g. I'm eating my favourite meal *right now*; I'm eating my favourite meal *in my favourite restaurant*.

auxiliary verb   A primary or modal verb which accompanies a main verb to clarify or add meaning (e.g. I *am* going; I *will* go).

clause   A sentence or a grammatical unit within a sentence which must (normally) consist of both a subject element and a verb element.

co-ordinating conjunction   The words *and/but/or* which are used to connect co-ordinating clauses in a sentence.

complex sentence   A sentence made up of one main (independent) clause plus one or more subordinate clauses (e.g. Because it was raining, I picked up my umbrella before I went out).

compound/co-ordinate sentence   A sentence made up of two or more independent clauses joined by co-ordinating conjunctions or semi-colons (e.g. It was raining and I took my umbrella out).

compound-complex sentence   A sentence made up from more than one main (independent) clause and several subordinate clauses (e.g. Because it was raining, I took my umbrella and I rang Robert before I went out).

concord   Grammatical agreement; the subject and verb should agree in number, (e.g. *That was* a mistake, not *That were* a mistake).

conjunction   The class of words such as *and/but/or* which connect clauses in a sentence. See **co-ordinating** and **subordinating conjunctions**.

connective   The function of words such as *and/but/or* which connect clauses in a sentence.

declarative   The most common written type of sentence which declares or states something (e.g. It's very cold outside).

demonstrative pronouns   Pronouns which indicate proximity (e.g. this/these, that/those).

determiner   Words that indicate the scope of a noun (e.g. a, the, that, some, any).

direct object   The person/thing directly affected by the action of the verb (e.g. I'm eating *my favourite meal* right now).

embedding   Inserting one grammatical unit within another (e.g. That postman, *who lost my parcel*, is very careless).

exclamative   The type of sentence which exclaims or expresses with emphasis (e.g. I'm freezing to death!).

finite verbs   Finite verb forms are fixed to a person, number and tense (e.g. *I love you* is singular and in the present tense). See also **non-finite verbs**.

genre   Categories of literature (e.g. poetry, novel, drama) which can be broken down into sub-genres such as Gothic, Realist Novel, Crime Fiction, Magic Realism, Romance etc. These categories relate to form, content and function, and may overlap.

idiom   A phrase with a meaning not easily determined from the constituent parts (e.g. get the sack).

imperative   The type of sentence which commands or requests something (e.g. shut the door).

indefinite article   The determiners *a* and *an*.

indirect object   The person/thing that is the indirect recipient of the action of the verb (e.g. My husband made my favourite meal for *me*).

interrogative   The type of sentence which asks a question (e.g. Are you cold?).

interrogative pronouns   More or less the same words as relative pronouns but are used to ask questions (e.g. *Whose* bag is that? *Which* book is yours?).

intransitive/transitive verbs   Intransitive verbs do not need to be followed by a direct object (e.g. I run) but transitive verbs do (e.g. I love *you*). Many verbs can be either intransitive or transitive (e.g. I smoke, or I smoke Cuban cigars).

linking/copular verbs   A small group of verbs such as to be, to go, to get, which link a subject and its complement (e.g. They *were* angry, I *got* angry).

main clause   The clause or clauses in a sentence which are independent and could stand alone grammatically.

metalanguage   The language used to describe language (*meta* comes from the Greek word for above).

modal verb   The following verbs which can be added to a full verb to express either probability or obligation: can, could, will, would, shall, should, may, might, must (e.g. He *should* go).

modifiers (pre-modifiers, post-modifiers)   Words in a noun phrase before or after the head noun which are grammatically dependent on it and alter or modify its meaning. For instance, in the noun phrase 'that chic little skirt in the window' there are pre-modifiers before the noun 'skirt' and post-modifiers after it.

nominal clause   A clause which replaces subject or object elements in a sentence (e.g. *I really like your outfit* with a nominal clause becomes *I really like what you are wearing*).

non-finite verbs   Non-finite verb forms are not limited to a person, number or tense. They are found in three forms: –ed (e.g *Excited* about meeting him, she arrived far too early); –ing (e.g. *Working* away from home, she was often lonely); and infinitive (e.g. I really want *to finish* that essay on time).

noun   Words that name persons/places/things or abstractions (e.g. Edward, Tanzania, guitar, happiness).

object complement   The part of the clause that adds meaning to the direct object (e.g. He found the chocolate *too sweet*).

open/closed class words   Nouns, adjectives, adverbs and verbs are called open word classes because they are evolving and expanding in number as language changes with society. Pronouns, conjunctions, determiners and prepositions generally do not change or increase in number.

parallelism   Repeated sentence constructions in a paragraph.

periodic sentence   In a periodic sentence there is a substantial gap between the subject and the verb of the main clause (e.g. The man in the cinema, having struggled continually with his overwhelming feelings of sympathy for the lead character, finally wept).

personal pronouns   Words which identify speakers, addressees and others (I, you, she, it, we, they).

phrase   The term phrase means a cluster of two or more words in a sentence, but differs from a clause because it lacks the essential subject + verb structure of the clause.

possessive pronouns   Pronouns which express ownership (my, your, hers etc.) act as determiners in the noun phrase; mine, yours, hers etc. are used on their own.

preposition   Words that express a relationship between nouns or other word classes, often of space or time (e.g. in, on, at, below, behind).

primary verb   The verbs to be, to have and to do which can be used either as full verbs (e.g. I *am* sad) or as auxiliary verbs attached to full verbs (e.g. Rosie *has* read all of Trollope's novels).

pronoun   Words used instead of a noun or noun phrase (e.g. it, he, who, theirs).

reciprocal pronouns   Pronouns used to express a two-way relationship (e.g. each other, one another).

reflexive pronouns   Pronouns which end in –self or –selves (e.g. myself, yourself, themselves).

regular/irregular verbs   The forms of a regular verb are governed by rules; an irregular verb is one where some of the forms are unpredictable (e.g. to bring). Usually verbs have '–ed' added to put them in the past tense; to bring is therefore an irregular verb because the past tense is not *I bringed* but *I brought*.

relative clause   A relative clause is a dependent clause which modifies the noun/noun phrase which precedes it (e.g. The tickets *that you wanted* are sold out).

relative pronouns   A small group of words that introduce relative clauses (who, whom, whose, which, that).

semantics   The study of linguistic meanings.

subject   The agent in the clause made up of a noun or noun phrase; the element in the sentence that controls the verb (e.g. *The man in the cinema* wept).

subject complement   The part of the clause that gives definition to the subject (e.g. My dinner was *absolutely delicious*).

subordinate clause   A clause which is dependent upon another grammatically (e.g. *Because he came too early*, nobody was in. We came home, *after he left*).

subordinating conjunction   A conjunction such as until, because, if, or when, which connects a subordinate clause to other clauses in a sentence.

syntax   The study of sentence structure, including word structure.

topic sentence   A sentence, often but not always the first, which states the key points considered in a paragraph.

verb A word or phrase which expresses the action, process or state in the clause (e.g. I'*m eating* my favourite meal right now; I *will go* to that football match; I *went* quietly).

FURTHER READING

Bryson, Bill (1990) *Mother Tongue: The English Language*. Harmondsworth: Penguin.
Brown, K. and Miller, J. (1991) *Syntax: A Linguistic Introduction to Sentence Structure*. London: Routledge.
Cameron, Deborah (1990) *The Feminist Critique of Language*. London: Routledge.
Carter, R. and Simpson, P. (eds) (1989) *Language, Discourse and Literature*. London: Unwin Hyman Ltd.
Carter, R. and Nash, W. (1990) *Seeing Through Language*. Oxford: Blackwell.
Crystal, David (1987) *Cambridge Encyclopedia of Language*. Cambridge: Cambridge University Press.
Crystal, David (1995) *Cambridge Encyclopedia of the English Language*. Cambridge: Cambridge University Press.
Crystal, David (1996) *Rediscover Grammar*. Harlow: Longman.
Coulthard, M. (ed.) (1994) *Advances in Written Text Analysis*. London: Routledge.
Fabb, Nigel (1994) *Sentence Structure*. London: Routledge.
Graddol, D., Cheshire, J. and Swann, J. (1994) *Describing Language*. Buckingham: Open University Press.
Harrison, Nancy (1985) *Writing English: A User's Manual*. The Croom Helm Communication Series, London: Routledge.
Hall, Nigel and Robinson, Anne (1996) *Learning About Punctuation*. Clevedon: Multilingual Matters.
Haynes, J. (1995) *Style*. London: Routledge.
Hoey, M. (1991) *Patterns of Lexis in Text*. Oxford: Oxford University Press.
Leech, Geoffrey (1989) *An A–Z of English Grammar and Usage*. London: Edward Arnold.
Jarvie, Gordon (1992) *Chambers Good Punctuation Guide*. Edinburgh: Chambers.
McDermott, John (1990) *Punctuation for Now*. Basingstoke: Macmillan.
Pope, Rob (1995) *Textual Intervention*. London: Routledge.
Salkie, R. (1995) *Text and Discourse Analysis*. London: Routledge.
Tannen, D. (ed.) (1993) *Framing and Discourse*. Cambridge: Cambridge University Press.
Yale, George (1985) *The Study of Language*. Cambridge: Cambridge University Press.

INDEX